DETOUR THROUGH DANGER

DETOUR

THROUGH

DANGER

The 1949 Journal of
R. LaVerne Morse

Compiled by Marcia Morse Odor

XULON PRESS

Xulon Press
2301 Lucien Way #415
Maitland, FL 32751
407.339.4217
www.xulonpress.com

© 2022 by Marcia Morse Odor

All rights reserved solely by the author. The author guarantees all contents are original and do not infringe upon the legal rights of any other person or work. No part of this book may be reproduced in any form without the permission of the author.

Due to the changing nature of the Internet, if there are any web addresses, links, or URLs included in this manuscript, these may have been altered and may no longer be accessible. The views and opinions shared in this book belong solely to the author and do not necessarily reflect those of the publisher. The publisher therefore disclaims responsibility for the views or opinions expressed within the work.

Unless otherwise indicated, Scripture quotations taken from the King James Version (KJV) – *public domain.*

Scripture quotations taken from the Holy Bible, New International Version (NIV). Copyright © 1973, 1978, 1984, 2011 by Biblica, Inc.™. Used by permission. All rights reserved.

Photos: © 2016 by R. LaVerne Morse

Cover Design: Karis Pratt, karisma-design.com

Editing: Karis Pratt, Marcia Morse Odor, Kent Odor, Lois Morse

Paperback ISBN-13: 978-1-66286-000-3
Ebook ISBN-13: 978-1-66286-001-0

Table of Contents

Preface	xiii
Introduction	1

PART I
China Journal   7

  Chapter 1
    Letter, Inoculations, and Vaccinations   8

  Chapter 2
    Pan American Clipper   17

  Chapter 3
    Flight to Interior China   23

  Chapter 4
    Communist and Tibetan Turmoil   29

  Chapter 5
    Negotiations and Finances   33

  Chapter 6
    Mission Home Base   37

  Chapter 7
    Dangers Looming All Around   41

PART II
Operation Rescue — 45

Chapter 1
What is the Atlantic Pact? — 46

Chapter 2
Dysentery and Delays — 49

Chapter 3
Flying Blind over Mountains—First Rescue — 53

Chapter 4
Tommy Guns and Confiscations—Second Rescue — 61

Chapter 5
Red Star Caps—Third Rescue — 65

Chapter 6
The Rest of the Story—Tighter Than a Drum — 70

PART III
Westward Toward Tibet — 79

Chapter 1
Recognition Granted and Plans Made — 80

Chapter 2
Stowaway at 6,400 Feet — 86

Chapter 3
Chengtu—Roast Duck and Rickety Rickshaws — 89

Chapter 4
Westward — 94

Chapter 5
Gorges, Rocky Cliffs, and *Reader's Digest* — 98

PART IV
Plateau Journal   103

Chapter 1
Preparations and Good Fortune   104

Chapter 2
Pangda Caravan and *Reader's Digest*   108

Chapter 3
Litang—14,000 Feet   116

Chapter 4
A New Caravan and 60 Loaded Yaks   122

Chapter 5
Batang Apples, Chinese Cookies, and Walnuts   131

PART V
Tibetan Journal   137

Chapter 1
Farewell Batang   138

Chapter 2
Past Border Hurdles   142

Chapter 3
Halted by Tibetan Military   147

Chapter 4
Pseudo-Shangri-La   151

Chapter 5
"The Gospel in Tibet?"   154

Chapter 6
Permission Granted!   160

Chapter 7
Markam Fort—Horns, Flutes, and Drums ... 163

Chapter 8
Privileged Travelers in Tibet ... 167

Chapter 9
Devil Dance ... 177

Chapter 10
Bandit Territory ... 160

Chapter 11
Five Stunned Brigands ... 183

Chapter 12
Communist-Tibetan Football ... 187

PART VI
The Salween Valley ... 193

Chapter 1
The Salween Situation ... 194

Chapter 2
Adverse Ideas ... 197

Chapter 3
Final Detour Through Danger ... 202

Epilogue ... 205

About R. LaVerne Morse ... 211

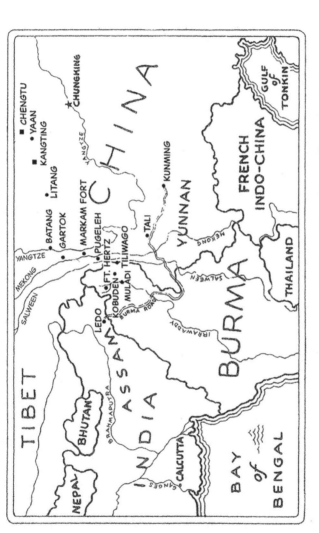

1949 —Map adapted from The Lookout

Preface

It was June 1949, and China was closing. The country of China was on the doorstep of a revolution that would change world history. Communism was coming.

After World War II ended, the Communist Revolution led by Mao Zedong began a scourge that slaughtered tens of millions of Chinese people and expelled and imprisoned thousands of foreigners, including many Americans and missionaries. Evacuating safely was foremost in all foreigners' minds. Gone were the days of hope and peace. Despair and fear filled the minds of everyone within the Chinese borders. The world watched from afar, heartbroken.

Russell LaVerne Morse, just 20 years old at the time, would make a decision that would shape the course of his life. He was a college student in Minnesota, but he had grown up in China until the age of 14. His parents, brothers, and sister were still there. He received a letter from his father urging him to come quickly to rejoin the family.

With the impending overthrow of the government, he could be a source of help for both his family and the mission there. If he could help, he had to come now!

Without hesitation, he hurriedly put a plan into motion to join the family.

Once in China, the family decided to travel west and establish a new mission station in the remote northern tip of Burma. LaVerne and his friend Mel traveled through forbidden Tibet into Burma to reach the family.

The six-month journey over the high mountain passes led to:

Hardship met with grit . . . through great danger . . . escaping the Communists . . .

Adventure harnessed with enthusiasm . . . through unknown lands and the Tibetan plateau . . .

And an unshakable faith that God would provide a way!

Introduction

The 20-year-old author of this story was no stranger to dangerous adventures. He learned at a very early age that dangerous living was to be expected as normal. Russell LaVerne Morse was the third son to missionaries J. Russell and Gertrude Morse, who set the direction of an adventurous life for their family as they left the United States with their firstborn, six-month-old Eugene, in 1921. They traveled six months by ship, train, and caravan to reach eastern Tibet before the year's end.

LaVerne was himself a newborn in 1929 when he was carried to China from California aboard a ship. Through more travel and dangers, the family planted themselves in the mountainous, undeveloped region of western China to do missionary work. Their hearts' desire was to share the love of God with those who had never had the chance to hear about His goodness.

When LaVerne was one year old, he came down first with pneumonia and then, before recovering, fell victim to a measles epidemic as well. His mother Gertrude feared for his life.

At age two, he survived a flu epidemic that took the lives of 100 members of the village where his family was stationed. As a child, he witnessed the deaths of neighbors and coworkers as other diseases passed through the region. Sickness was constant; the danger of disease was all around. Having completed a six-week medical training course, LaVerne's father was the most medically qualified person around. The mission's supply of medicines served everyone in the area.

This stark region with no amenities of any kind was the playground for LaVerne's developmental years. Danger was everywhere in the mountainous terrain and deep gorges but climbing up and down the mountainsides on footpaths was just his daily life. Experiences with animals, both domesticated and wild, were daily occurrences. Law and order were very much like that of the wild American West—everyone was responsible for his own safety.

At age 10, while his father and brothers were away, LaVerne, his sister Ruth Margaret, and his mother miraculously escaped in the middle of the night as their house was swept from underneath them in a flash flood. Despite having lost everything, the family relocated to a new station in a new valley and continued their missionary work with barely a pause. LaVerne and Ruth were sent to a boarding school in Tali near the famous Burma Road.

Introduction

In the early 1940s the Japanese invaded and bombed China, killing millions. War surrounded the area of the family's mission. On the other side of the world, the Japanese bombed Pearl Harbor on December 7, 1941.

In 1941, the Japanese bombed the area of the boarding school that 12-year-old LaVerne and his sister Ruth attended. They escaped into tunnels which led to caves in the mountain. For the next two years, LaVerne's schooling was comprised of reading a set of encyclopedias.

As a developing young teen, LaVerne was willing and able to take large amounts of responsibility. He spoke four languages, and occasionally preached sermons from the Bible in churches the family had established.

By the mid-1940s, the Morse family had seen amazing success in their missionary work among the Lisu people—thousands had become believers. The family had experienced fruit of their diligent work and demonstrated the courage to live through the dangers that were all around them. They would endure any hardship to live among the people they chose to love and share the testimony of God's love.

At age 14, LaVerne set out with his two older brothers, Robert (age 17) and Eugene (age 20), to secure food and supplies. The family had been cut off from the outside world unable to receive any resources or communications because of the war. The brothers left on their 30-day journey by first visiting and encouraging church leaders along the way. Their destination was Fort Hertz, the base airfield of the Allied Forces. It was the staging area for air missions over the "Hump"—what the WWII Allies called the eastern end of the Himalayan mountains. It was over these mountains they flew supplies from India to China, to support the Chinese in their battles against the Japanese occupation. The brothers' adventure took them over an 11,000-foot, snow-covered pass in the Salween-Irrawaddy Range and then down into the Putao plain of Northern Burma, through both the bitter cold of the snowy mountains and the steamy tropical jungle of the valley.

As the boys entered the valley, they contracted malaria and arrived at the base deathly ill. The commander realized they were a resource of valuable information, having just come from the areas where planes were going down and pilots were being lost. The commander immediately put them on a flight to Assam, India, to recover in a British hospital and be debriefed about their knowledge of the regions of their travels.

As they all recovered, it was decided that LaVerne should be enrolled in a boarding school in India at the border of Nepal. After one month, not wanting to stay at the school, he penned letters of application to the U.S. Army and the British Royal Air Force, volunteering to serve as a guide—he knew the areas and spoke many of the languages. He had turned 15 on the journey, but both branches of the Allied Forces rejected him because of his young age.

Feeling disheartened, LaVerne received a letter from his aunt in America with a check to pay the school fees.

Introduction

With those funds in hand, he left the school and traveled alone for six weeks, across India from the far northeast near Nepal to the southwest coast until he reached Bombay—a journey of 1,000 miles. At the harbor he found a freighter unloading U.S. Army supplies for the troops fighting the war in Burma and China. When he learned that the ship would be returning to Los Angeles and had space for boarders, he secured a berth.

LaVerne was a passenger aboard that freighter for almost a year, traveling to the U.S. by the long route (necessary to bypass the Japanese submarines). He sailed into the Antarctic Ocean twice, around both Africa and South America. Because communication had been cut off, this journey happened without his parents knowing where he was or what he was doing.

At the harbor of Los Angeles, the Red Cross was summoned to help him enter the U.S. as an unaccompanied minor. Forwarding agents from a supporting church in southern California received him and then sent him on a train to his grandmother and aunt in Tulsa, Oklahoma, where he completed his high school education. Upon graduation he enrolled in Minnesota Bible College in Rochester, Minnesota.

As he was finishing the second semester of his second year of college, Russell LaVerne Morse made a decision that would take him back into the thick of danger once again.

PART I
China Journal

It was 1949. LaVerne, a college student in Minnesota, received a letter from his missionary father, J. Russell Morse, in China. "Well, LaVerne, be forewarned before you decide. The years ahead of us are very likely to be even more dangerous and fraught with hardships than our past 28 years. But the period ahead will also be a great opportunity to prove and demonstrate the power of the living God, and to win great victories for the glory of His name...."

Chapter 1

Letter, Inoculations, and Vaccinations

*P*lans have been made and carried out so rapidly within the past six weeks that I still can hardly believe I am not dreaming. From being in Bible college in Minneapolis and planning to enter the Summer Institute of Linguistics [a special course for Bible translating] in Oklahoma, to being at the mission station in Kunming, China, and preparing here for several years of immediate missionary work where China, Tibet, and Burma meet—such has been the development of the past six weeks.

On May 28, somewhat over a month ago, I received a letter from my father, J. Russell Morse, Kunming, China, with the following news:

> You can still get through to us if you streamline everything, get your Chinese, Hong Kong, and Philippine visas promptly, and

fly all the way to Hong Kong and Kunming, and then Likiang. In a week or less flying time, you could reach Likiang, beyond which would be the caravan journey to Ai-wa, and across the great pass to the village of Pugeleh in the Salween Valley. This is taking it for granted that Communist advances would not be so rapid as to knock out the use of airfields at Kunming and Likiang. . . .

But the advisability of your launching out on this certainly dangerous undertaking is something you will have to decide between yourself and our Lord. We can neither advocate nor oppose it but will pray for you in it. The China situation has all the experts puzzled, and few dare to predict what may develop. It, perhaps, depends on what will be the attitude and policy of the Chinese Communists, how far patterned after and in collusion with Communist Russia. The safest thing will be to keep out of their clutches until they have shown abundant proof of a change of heart.

On the border of anti-Communist Tibet and of remote and primitive extreme

Upper Burma, we may be able to do that with the collaboration of the Lisu and other Christians, but it is certain to be a very inconvenient and dangerous life, and it would be well to be a "Tarzan" in those jungles.

I believe that you would qualify better for the manifold phases of getting all this personnel and equipment through to Tibetan Lisuland. Both Eugene and Robert have worked so hard during furlough and on that neither has the strength and resistance he had last term. Although my strength is not equal to theirs, still my health is at least as good, my more than 20 years of experience in medical work is one indication that I can meet a special need there. Also, both Eugene and Robert will be more tied down by family responsibilities than before, and you will be free to be "trouble-shooter."

A very large proportion of the people in Tibetan Lisuland are still non-Christian, and among these the opium ring, the whiskey ring, and the officials who have always tried to exploit the tribespeople have always resented our being there and having so great an influence in the country.

With chaotic governmental conditions, then an anti-American and anti-Christian party coming into power and sending out new officials to take over, and our being so far removed from our own consular representatives, it is a question of how long we can remain even in the Salween Valley. Of course, the Inner Tibetans have already taken over Atuntze (five days' journey north of mission field), and the possibility of their coming down to take over Wei Hsi also would seal off all the Mekong Valley above there. Truly, we should be "lost horizon" more than ever. Communication with the outside world by mail or telegraph is quite likely to be cut off, but perhaps we might send letters to Myitkyina, Burma, which takes six or more weeks, and then post them onward from there.

Well, LaVerne, be forewarned before you decide. The years ahead of us are very likely to be even more dangerous and fraught with hardships than our past terms of 28 years. But the period ahead will also be a great opportunity to prove and demonstrate the power of the living God, and to win great victories for the glory of His name.

Laverne Morse

Letter from LaVerne's father

Letter, Inoculations, and Vaccinations

China Visa Granted

Having received this word from my father, I immediately began making definite preparations for going, praying that if it were God's will for me to go to the field immediately, as He seemed to be leading, the way would continue to be opened. It was possible to buy the comparatively few supplies which I would be able to bring on the plane, largely clothing, all within about a day.

On the evening of June 1, a cablegram arrived from my father in Kunming asking if I were able to obtain visas from the foreign government to enter China since, if not, he would continue up-country while transportation was still available. During those days, it seemed that almost any day the rest of China might be taken over by the Communists. The morning after I received the cablegram, my passport arrived back from the Chinese consulate-general with the visa for which I had applied for China residence. I was able to cable back that afternoon, "China visa granted."

With the aid of several very helpful schoolmates during the closing days of school, I was able to complete most of the correspondence and other business matters to be attended to before leaving the States. Also, upon receiving the Chinese visa so quickly (within about six days), I telephoned the Pan American Airways agent in Minneapolis for a reservation leaving from Los Angeles on June 13 to Hong Kong. To my surprise, he was able to confirm it immediately without even telegraphing the main office in San Francisco. It seemed that step by step the way was opening.

Inoculations

When I went to the Pan American office to buy my ticket on June 8, the agent asked me whether I had received all my inoculations and vaccinations. He said they generally took about 15 to 20 days. That was June 2, and I was due to leave on the 13th! I hurried to the doctor several blocks away. It was his day off, but I made an appointment for the next day. On June 3 the doctor was prepared to give me four different kinds of inoculations or vaccinations at once—smallpox, typhus, cholera, and typhoid-paratyphoid. He explained that the next in the series were supposed to be given seven and ten days apart. However, I could receive each of mine six days apart. Thus, I could carry the material for inoculations with me and could receive the next in Tulsa, and the last in Honolulu—just before leaving United States territory—while I would be there for about 20 hours between planes. Everything was still working out.

Pack and Pray

From Minneapolis, I proceeded to Tulsa, Oklahoma, to see the home folk there. Also, I stopped en route on

Letter, Inoculations, and Vaccinations

Sunday in Des Moines, Iowa, to speak at the College Avenue Church. In Tulsa the main task was packing to leave and storing almost all of my things from school, including all clothes which had to be dry cleaned. Almost a completely new set of washable clothes had to be bought, because on the mission field we do not have a dry cleaner around the corner. It was certainly good, too, to see Grandmother Morse still quite active and capable at the age of 88 years, and also Aunt Eva and various friends in Tulsa. It was especially hard to leave Grandmother, even though we do hope to see each other again in this world, the Lord willing.

During the past five years, ever since I came back to America at the age of 15, Grandmother, together with aunts Eva and Louise, has been truly wonderful to me. Their able and considerate advice, their interest and care, their help in all ways—all these made Tulsa home for me, first during the years when I was a student at Central High School, and then later when I was in Minnesota Bible College. I remember, too, the home-made fruitcakes Grandmother sent to me in college and how good they tasted.

From Tulsa, I flew to Los Angeles in a speedy DC-6 American Airliner in order to contact the British Consulate-General there for a transit visa for Hong Kong. That was the one major step yet before departure. Saturday morning, my host in Los Angeles, W. K. Chamberlain (the Chamberlains are friends of long standing), went with me on the all-important trip to the British Consulate-General.

Arriving there, we found that because of the refugee-crowded status of Hong Kong, all visas had to be applied for through the New York consulate. However, the consular official went on, he could telephone long-distance on Monday, to ask whether he could grant me a Hong Kong visa. Monday! It was Monday evening that I was due to fly to Hong Kong. There was still one door to be opened for my departure, and it was up to God's leading.

Sunday morning, then, I went on a Pacific Electric bus through the fruit lands of southern California to speak at San Bernardino for the morning service. After a very enjoyable visit there, Mr. and Mrs. Martin, from Compton, having come to San Bernardino to see me in the morning, took me to Long Beach to speak at the evening service in First Church there. The Chamberlains from Los Angeles, to my pleasant surprise, were at the evening service in Long Beach to take me back to their home after the service. I certainly appreciated all the kindness of each one of the wonderful friends in southern California.

Chapter 2

Pan American Clipper

With hearts beating a little faster than usual Monday morning, Mr. Chamberlain and I went to see the British Consulate-General. The consul put through his call, asked me to wait a few minutes, and soon came back to say with a smile that it was OK—I could go to Hong Kong. He stamped the visa into my passport, and I was ready to go.

Everything seemed a bit like a dream, but certainly there was no time for dreaming. That afternoon I did the last of the shopping. Packing presented only a few hours' job. I was able to take on the plane only the most essential items, about 100 pounds in baggage (besides about 30 pounds of coats and the heaviest items packed into ample coat pockets, all for me to "wear" in boarding the plane). About 4:45 p.m., the Chamberlains drove me through the busy Los Angeles streets to the Inglewood airport. Friends from Los Angeles, Long Beach, Alhambra, Pacific

Palisades, and Inglewood were at the airport. After the flight was called, just before I went through the gate to board the airplane, we all paused together for a word of prayer.

In the dusk of the evening, with the lights of the airfield all around, the Pan American Clipper warmed up the motors and taxied out to the main runway. At 7:54 p.m., June 13, it picked up speed down the runway with a roar and climbed upwards into the air. Up and up it went, out to sea. In a few moments it passed the curving line of lights along the ocean shore. The lights of the city behind grew dimmer and dimmer and disappeared as the huge plane climbed sharply into a layer of thick mist. In several minutes the airplane plowed through to the top of the clouds with the blue sky overhead. The engines roared reassuringly as the clipper headed towards the last glow of the sunset out over the Pacific. Soon it was dark. About midnight, though, I looked out through the porthole from my sleeperette to see the moonlight on the sea of fleecy white clouds below and into the horizon.

Pan American Clipper

Tropical Hawaii

Early in the morning after leaving southern California and the mainland of the U.S.A., the Pan American Clipper bound for Honolulu came in sight of a number of islands and fishing boats upon the waters below. About sunrise, the clipper circled downward near Diamond Head and landed at Honolulu airport. I disembarked with all my baggage into an environment of palm trees, tropical ocean, sky, and mountains. Around me were various outgoing passengers, almost without exception decorated with gorgeous multiflowered leis around their necks.

After cleaning up at the air terminal, getting a haircut, and finally realizing that I was in the Hawaiian Islands, I obtained transportation downtown. It was here that I got the last in the series of inoculations for departure. I did not exactly relish, of course, the necessity of inoculations with their resultant headaches when I wanted to enjoy all the new sights. However, when I went to the medical clinic to be "shot" twice, the doctor gave me some aspirin to relieve the after-effects, especially so that I could go swimming in the afternoon.

After doing some last-minute shopping in downtown Honolulu, I boarded a bus with "Waikiki" on it. At the famous beach by that name, I almost pickled my tonsils in the saturated salt water when I went out where the huge breakers were roaring in. Around 5:00 p.m., I returned to downtown Honolulu on the bus, had supper, and returned to the airport on the other side of town. When passengers were finally allowed to board the Hong Kong plane, I was so sleepy that I do not remember the plane's taking off. I was awakened briefly only when the stewardess or the steward asked to fix my seat into the sleeperette for more complete reclining.

The Pacific Islands

During the day of June 15–16 (a single day), I awoke in time to take pictures of Midway. All over the island, a U.S. government bird sanctuary, were birds, birds, and more birds. The most interesting were the huge baby albatrosses which practically dotted the island. One of these goose-sized, down-covered youngsters posed very charmingly while I took his picture from about three feet away. After the plane left Midway, there was a terrific waste of time: 24 hours were lost all within one second when the plane crossed the International Date Line.

About midafternoon, the plane came down to the desolate-looking coral island named Wake. It had not a single respectable tree on it—just big bushes all over. I did take a stroll along the beach and picked up some good specimens of coral, out of which the island is built from the ocean floor. The entire island was somewhat like a ring around a lagoon, with several breaks connecting the latter with the ocean. The shore, too, ran out fairly shallow a short distance, and then dropped precipitously into the turquoise-blue ocean.

On the beach was some of the wreckage from the war—an airplane propeller sticking out of the sand, burnt fabric and molten metal that apparently were flung from a disintegrating plane. When the Pan American Clipper "Ocean Express" taxied out for takeoff, passengers could see a red Japanese sun on a plane wing sticking out of the bushes. After the clipper took off, I looked back and saw a half-sunken ship a short way offshore.

Our plane droned on across the blue waters and stopped next in Guam, then Manila, and then flew over the Philippines. The clouds parted enough over Corregidor for the passengers to see the rugged outlines of that historic island. Then, finally, the plane was high over the South China Sea heading toward Hong Kong.

Hong Kong Airport

The Hong Kong airport is notorious as one of the worst of major airports, being surrounded by hills and mountains. It was near there that Quentin Roosevelt, nephew of Theodore Roosevelt, was killed some time ago because of poor visibility for his plane. Anyway, while we were still at sea, the clipper started circling. It did so for possibly 30 minutes to get below the dense clouds. By the time we finally were below the misty formations, we looked to be only 30 feet above the waves.

The plane headed toward the mainland and Hong Kong. Through breaks in the clouds, islands could be seen rising precipitously out of the sea. Then we had mountains on all sides. We zoomed along the face of a mountain, then tipped our wing as though to avoid scraping a hillside a few feet away. We dropped down beyond the hill on a runway which appeared altogether too short for the four-engined clipper. With brakes engaged seemingly as hard as possible, flaps down, the huge plane finally ground to a stop at the end of the runway a short distance from the waters of the bay.

Chapter 3

Flight to Interior China

In Hong Kong I was surprised to find a reservation made via China National Aviation Corporation (C.N.A.C.) to Kunming in the name of "J. R. Morse." I had asked from Manila for reservation on the first plane available, but couldn't figure out how C.N.A.C. acquired the initials "J.R." As I figured out later, my father had made advance reservation for me through the Kunming office. At any rate, from the airport a bus took me to the C.N.A.C. office at the Peninsula Hotel. There I sent a radiogram to my father telling of my upcoming arrival in Kunming on the next available plane at 12:45 p.m. on Sunday, June 19.

As to accommodations in Hong Kong, in the meantime, I found out hotel rooms were practically unavailable because of the crowded refugee situation. I had serious thoughts of sitting up several nights in the Peninsula Hotel lobby. Nevertheless, as I was preparing to telephone various hotels, I chatted a while with a C.N.A.C.

representative at the desk. Eventually the person said, "Oh, you are the passenger who was looking for a room? We can give you one at the Peninsula Hotel." I had already asked and been denied a room at the hotel desk, but apparently the airlines have rooms specifically reserved for their passengers. As a potential passenger, C.N.A.C. provided me one. I was quite pleasantly surprised to find such good accommodations—with a gorgeous view of Hong Kong harbor and private shower facilities—in which to unpack and clean up from the sweltering heat of Hong Kong. It seemed surely everything was continuing to work out.

Hong Kong—The British Gateway of the Orient

The following day I shopped for some supplies in Hong Kong, getting a little acquainted with that British gateway of the Orient. In the afternoon, I ascended the famous peak on the cable car that ascends possibly at a 45-degree angle in some places, and brings one down sitting backward. In just a few minutes, the cable car took its passengers from about 200 feet above sea level to 1,300 feet. Up on the peak, I enjoyed the scenery of the busy harbor with its many steamships, a few warships, and also the fern-covered tropical setting. The vegetation and mountainsides certainly resembled those of the Salween Valley.

Sunday morning, June 19, at 9:10, I arrived at the airport to hurry through formalities and pay for my fare. I had some difficulty with a cashier's check until the pilot of the plane, a very friendly American, reassured the Chinese staff at the C.N.A.C. office that the check was good. All in all, C.N.A.C. was very helpful, not even weighing my overweight baggage or taking note of possibly 40 pounds of coats (with pockets heavily and tightly packed) which I was wearing or carrying, and a number of hand parcels. The plane roared down the runway and over the hill at the end of it at about 10:30 a.m.

The flight to inland China was interesting, though the plane (DC-4) was w I was the only American aboard except the above-mentioned pilot, who had been in the Air Transport Command over the "Hump" [the eastern end of the Himalayas between India and China] during the war. He came back from the pilot's cabin at one time and discussed with me the "Hump," political situations in China, and so forth for possibly half an hour during the flight to Kunming. Every once in a while, he would look out at the clouds to make sure his Chinese co-pilot and the flight engineer were directing the plane properly.

Arrival in Kunming

After five hours of flying above the many clouds, and occasionally peering down through breaks at the hills, mountains, rivers, and rice fields of China, the passengers finally noticed a large lake below. This turned out to be the lake near Kunming. The plane dropped toward it, circled far out and down, and then came into the landing strip. In seconds it had rolled to a stop and the passengers were pouring out: Kunming, at last. Five days before I had been in Los Angeles, California; now I was in inland China.

Looking out of the porthole at the crowd meeting the plane, I glimpsed my father, mother, sister, and the recent missionary recruits who had come out earlier this year—Miss Lora Banks and Miss Imogene Williams. The look of eager expectation on the faces of all of them seemed to darken to concern as they watched more and more passengers come out, but not LaVerne. I was putting on all my three coats, carrying another coat over my arm, and gathering the various handbags and parcels.

Finally, I emerged to relieve their increasing anxiety. It was surely wonderful to see them all again and looking so well. Going to the customs inspection, I was introduced to a friend or two of Daddy's—including the chief customs inspector. My army-style B4 bag, duffle bag, parcels, coats (including everything in my coat pockets)—a total of about 120 pounds—were all quickly passed. The group of us rode to town in a rickety C.N.A.C. bus, and then took rickshaws—my first ride in such for about six years—to the mission home in the Shang Hsipa suburb of Kunming.

That evening at the Sunday church service of the Church of Christ in Shang Hsipa, I was introduced to the congregation. One week before, I had spoken in First Church in Long Beach, California. This Sunday I was with a congregation of Chinese brethren in inland China.

When in 1941 I emerged from the interior to Kunming for several days, the city looked very modern to me. However, now it looks strangely different. There is a multitude of odors which one smells along cobblestoned and muddy streets. I hope to get a picture of the Morse family trotting to town in the "suburban bus," a two-wheeled horse-cart with three rows of hard seats which seem very unspringy as the tiny pony drags the cart over the bumps and ruts. The country is picturesque, but—oh, me!—so very dirty, tumbled-down, and ancient. One cannot imagine inland China until he sees it. Regarding the languages, though I have kept up well with the Lisu language, having taught it in Minnesota Bible College, I had forgotten much of the Chinese. However, it is coming back rapidly day by day.

J. Russell and Gertrude in a horse cart

The month since my arrival has gone by rapidly and well-filled. I had not expected to be in Kunming so long before continuing up-country to the interior. Now, though, because of the new requirement of obtaining residence permits for the Burmese sector of our mission field, it will be at least several weeks yet before any of us here can continue up-country.

Chapter 4

Communist and Tibetan Turmoil

The Communists have not taken over here by the end of June as we had expected. Nevertheless, many political bombs have been exploding round about. Reports from up-country reveal developments there unexpectedly much more severe than in Kunming. In the Upper Salween Valley, the magistrate heard that one of the local Chinese leaders was plotting to establish an "independent" government. He promptly sent soldiers to execute the potential rebel. However, other rebels in turn rose up against the magistrate. The latter fled from the valley, being stripped of goods and arms on the way out.

The newly instated "independent" group (possibly instigated by a few Communists) threatened the Christians of the Salween Valley that they would destroy the chapels and would force them to plant opium, work on Sundays, and discontinue church services. They also demanded to search our mission house at Tada, in which our supplies were locked when the family went to the United States on furlough. Temporarily, at least, the potential "searchers" were bluffed off by the elders of the Tada congregation.

Killing, Burning, and Looting

In the Mekong Valley, where most of the missionaries were at last report, a similar independent Communist group confiscated Isabel Dittemore's .38 revolver. They also demanded money from my brother Robert and his wife Betty, with threats of search and confiscation. However, after "contributing" $50 silver "for support of the forces of peace," they were, for the time being, on good terms with the insurgents. Later, it was reported that at Yea Chi, a day's journey north from where the missionaries were located, "independent" elements rebelled against the *tusi* or petty king of that region. They burned his several extensive "palaces." "The tusi—an old but energetic character—" fled northward and aroused a tribe of war-loving border Tibetans who were his allies.

"With the tusi in the lead," a horde of rugged, merciless Tibetan horsemen swarmed southward. The Chinese of Yea Chi thereupon killed all of his family except his son's wife, who escaped severely wounded. The Tibetans advanced to Yea Chi and "cleaned up" on the Chinese— killing, burning, and looting. Nine-tenths of Yea Chi is thus reported to be laid waste. One of our Chinese Christian friends here, Li Chao Fung, was worried about his family in Yea Chi until he heard they had escaped just several hours ahead of the Tibetans. The Tibetan plunderers reportedly went south on the east bank of the Mekong River at least to Ai-wa. Robert and Betty, Mrs. Isabel Dittemore, and Jane Kinnett are all on the west side of the river from Ai-wa. So, we believe that the Tibetans were not able to get dugout canoes or intact bamboo rope bridges to cross the river, which is in full flood all summer. Thus, we have been constantly and earnestly praying for the safety of all of them.

Eugene and Helen

On the way to Lisuland, Eugene and his wife Helen, with two-month-old David Lowell, flew to Likiang on May 19. However, because of the unsettled conditions up-country, they were unable to get caravan horses until July 21. Meanwhile, about July 1, the countryside around the city of Likiang was stirred up according to the pattern of Communist tactics elsewhere. Reportedly over 10,000 country people swarmed into the city, deposed the district government, confiscated arms of the militia, and set up an independent government.

The first piece of news indicated simply a people's overthrow of oppressing officials. However, after discussing travel plans with Eugene via telegraph, he said, "Our geraniums are vermillion, recogitate." In other words, the recently installed government is bright red, so think over implications. Whatever the case, we are praying for them amidst the fighting, turmoil, and dangers which we can only guess about. Above all, we know that He who said, "Lo, I am with you always, even unto the end of the world," is still the same today as He has been throughout all these years.

Chapter 5

Negotiations and Finances

While in Kunming, the main objective before any of us depart for "where China, Tibet, and Burma meet" is obtaining official recognition for our mission work in northernmost Burma and securing permanent residence permits for members of the mission in that area. About half of the entire mission field is in the extreme northeast jungles and mountains of Kachin State, Burma, just south of Inner Tibet. So far, none of the mission has resided permanently over there because of the unhealthful climate of rain and steaming heat. Mosquitoes in their millions carry malarial germs. Except for several kinds of grain, practically all food has to be brought in from the China side. Thus, members of the mission have gone over there for only a few months at a time.

Now, however, the tribespeople throughout the area to the borders of India and Inner Tibet have been so responsive and so urgent in requests for us to come to them that we hope several members of the Morse family may settle permanently there.

In the past, when the British ruled Burma, we were not required to have permits and visas for entrance. But in the general wave of independence for Asiatic countries, Burma became a separate, autonomous nation, and we now need official permits in order to continue our work. This may involve prolonged negotiations, but it is essential since it may determine the fate of the entire Burma work, including over 35 Churches of Christ. Thus, my father and I have been negotiating through the Burmese and American consulates in Kunming, the American Embassy in Rangoon, and directly with the Foreign Office of the Union of Burma.

Financial Problems on Mission Field

Another important activity in preparation for going up-country, and probably the most tedious, has been getting silver money. Part of it is for ourselves; part is for the others up-country. Exchanging is a very complicated process. First of all, the exchange rate may vary so much against the U.S. dollar from day to day that one may lose several hundred silver dollars by exchanging either a day early or a day late. For instance, the exchange of Yunnan silver (clumsy half-dollar pieces only) to one U.S. dollar was $4.30 when I first arrived. Some days later, it dipped to $3.80 silver to one U.S. dollar. Now, it has recovered to about $4.10.

Even with the varying rates it isn't possible simply to exchange at any bank. Rather, one must know the dispensary operators, photographic shops, etc., which will want to have U.S. bank drafts for use in their trade. They may want to exchange only a comparative little at a time, perhaps U.S. $50. Because silver for use up-country is available only here in Kunming, I have had to get over 30 times that amount for the various missionaries.

Furthermore, the natives up-country are suspicious of the coins lest they be merely silver-plated copper. Thus, new silver is practically useless. Well-used pieces, ones that have been tested by use, are necessary. Old pieces must still be in comparatively good condition with all inscriptions legible, and the coins must all "ring" true. [True silver has a ring when it is spun on the table; copper has a dull sound.] Because of such requirements, only about 60 percent of the silver bought here is suitable for Tibetan Lisuland. The rest must be used locally or exchanged for another lot. Consequently, I have gone downtown many days in succession to get the needed silver.

You can imagine the problems of sorting 18,000 silver half-dollars. To carry them around is about like carrying lead. You can picture me sitting cross-legged on the floor in my room, hour after hour, ringing silver pieces. After final testing, all the money has to be counted and recounted and wrapped in paper and in cloth. Lastly, it has to be tied securely in rolls of $100 each to prevent its breaking loose and jingling in the boxes during the long caravan journey.

Now at last, all of the silver is acquired and stored near my bed. With robbers breaking into houses every few nights, I feel like someone sleeping atop a box of dynamite with the fuses connected.

Chapter 6

Mission Home Base

It's a gorgeous day here in the Kunming plain. In spite of its being summer, the weather has been comfortably cool. Although Kunming's latitude is about that of Cuba, the 6,400-foot elevation gives it a climate which I believe could compete favorably with any in the United States, even in California. The sun is shining brightly today amidst stretches of billowy snow-white clouds and clear blue sky. All around the plain are the mountains with clouds nestling around their tops.

I am seated upstairs at my desk in this comparatively well-built Yunnan-Tibetan Christian Mission Home. Outside one window, the tall bamboo trees are waving in the gentle breeze at the edge of the lawn, next to a clump of broad-leafed banana trees. Down the walk, beside several recently transplanted apple trees, are two palm trees near the brook which flows through the mission compound. Birds of various sorts are singing, twittering, cawing, and chirping.

Next door, in contrast to the church services in this compound, the neighbors are in the midst of five days of Confucius ceremonies. Cymbals are clanging, drums beating, and shrill horns blowing their meager range of eerie notes. Through another window from the house, one can see across the green rice fields to downtown Kunming with the hills and mountains beyond. About a mile to the west is the large Kunming Lake with its sampans and two paddle-wheel steamers.

Whereas Daddy and I have been working on and are now waiting for the Burmese permits, there is also an abundance of other useful activity for us here at Kunming. The fairly new work of the Yunnan-Tibetan Christian Mission in the Shang Hsipa suburb has prospered.

Just last Sunday afternoon, about 20 of the congregation and we missionaries went in a Chinese sampan on Kunming Lake for a baptismal service. We directed the boat out to a fairly clean but shallow place. While the rest of us watched from the boat, Chinese evangelist Mr. Peter C. Yin baptized three persons according to the New Testament pattern. There are unlimited opportunities for evangelistic work in the many villages around here.

J. Russell in Kunming

The present chapel is far too small for potential audiences. If the political troubles in China were to be settled, we would surely commence immediately with construction of a more adequate house of worship. We are praying that the present Christians may be steadfast in all political events, and that the work may continue to grow. One family recently burned all its idols. The yet-unbelieving neighbors then began persecuting the members of that family in petty ways, attributing any small misfortunes that befell them to the wrath of evil spirits. Several days ago, the village leaders tried to force them to donate money for incense to the community's Buddhist rainy-season ceremonies. They steadfastly refused.

Interest has increased steadily. Mother does home visitation in the nearby communities throughout the week and holds night classes several times a week for people who want to become Christians. Also, she and the new missionaries have been conducting a Bible training school for the English-speaking Christian leaders of this Kunming work. All these developments and the continued receptiveness of the people make me hope great things for the future.

I have also been having some lessons in the Chinese language since arriving. Bargaining for prices downtown, being among the Chinese, and having to speak their language and taking notes on the services at the church have all helped me to remember much of the partly forgotten Chinese language. On July 31, I am due to deliver my first sermon in Chinese; I am preparing for that occasion with anticipation and a tinge of dread.

LaVerne in Kunming

Chapter 7

Dangers Looming All Around

*I*n Kunming there is a very uneasy peace with dangers looming all around the horizon. Fighting was reported the other day, within possibly 30 miles of Kunming between Communist hands and Nationalist soldiers. Meanwhile, Daddy and I are preparing while we wait for further developments regarding the Burmese permits and regarding our continuing—perhaps Mother and my adopted Chinese sister Drema Esther also with us—to the main part of the work up-country "where China, Tibet, and Burma meet." More and more, we feel the need of prayers.

Evacuation Begins

Sometime past, the family had decided it best for my sister Ruth Margaret (14 years old) to return to the States for high school. Especially when the Communists crossed the

Yangtze River, and many of the missionaries in South China started evacuating. On advice of the American Consulate, the Kunming American School, a small but efficient organization primarily for missionary children, was disbanded.

The question was, "Where should Ruth go to school in the States?" The problem was solved when Helen Myers Morse's parents, Mr. and Mrs. Oscar L. Myers of Terre Haute, Indiana, graciously offered to take Ruth practically as one of their children. We were all greatly pleased that Ruth could be with so wonderful and talented a Christian family.

We arranged for Ruth to travel with one of the teachers from the Kunming American School, who was going back to the States with three other students being returned by their parents. Then, we heard that the United States Government was making a special offer to evacuate from Hong Kong to the States by airplane for only $380, less even than the cheapest boat fare.

Finally, all arrangements were made for Ruth and the rest. On the morning of July 15, about 35 missionaries and their families gathered at the airport. Everyone was milling around at the edge of the bleak airstrip taking pictures and doing last-minute visiting. It was hard to say goodbye to Ruth; it might be several years before we would see her again. All the passengers boarded the plane, and soon it was taxiing to the takeoff strip, us waving to them and them to us. Tears flowed as the plane roared down the runway and lifted into the air.

Six years ago, when I was Ruth's age, I left for the States under similar circumstances. Now, I had just recently come back to the mission field, but Ruth was leaving to go to school with its preparations for future service.

Back in the States, I appreciated the loving care of relatives, the kindness of friends, and the wonderful fellowship of the churches. I asked that God grant to Ruth the same opportunities for development and service, the same Christian fellowship that would never be forgotten. We watched the plane, only a black dot by now against the white clouds in the distance, swing eastward over the mountains toward Hong Kong on its long journey across the Pacific to America.

Ruth Margaret's departure

PART II
Operation Rescue

August of 1949. Panic has stricken China! Communist armies are advancing toward Kunming. Flights out of China are closing. All Americans are authorized by the U.S. State Department to leave China. Communications are poor and under censorship. LaVerne's brother Eugene and his family are stuck in Likiang with Communist soldiers one day's travel away. A rescue mission unfolds involving Laverne, his friend Mel, and his father, J. Russell Morse.

Chapter 1

What is the Atlantic Pact?

Several days ago—or was it just yesterday?—I embarked on a project I've now dubbed "Operation Rescue." (Another option was "Operation Scarface," like the nickname given the Likiang Snow Peak during the past World War by American aviators.)

Eugene and Helen with baby David Lowell had been held up in Likiang when the Communist turnover came. When they had attempted to proceed to the mission field up-country and had traveled two days' journey from Likiang to Shigu, Communist soldiers forced them to turn back to Likiang, where they were held almost as prisoners and where their goods, carried on 35 horses, were searched, and much equipment was "confiscated" by the Communists according to their individual whims.

They were kept in Likiang with the hope that eventually they might be able to proceed up-country with the permission of the hammer and sickle. Meanwhile, they were behind a virtual iron curtain, without knowledge of the worsening international and outside situations. Their radio had been seized, and the only news allowed to circulate was that of Communist propaganda. By our telegrams, we were able to give them practically no information since we knew everything was under censorship.

On August 19, a secret session was called by the American Consulate for all the missions in Kunming in which there were American nationals represented. This was the group that the consulate had been authorized by the State Department to move out of Kunming in the near future before the city turned altogether red. Thus, with the international and local situations very critical, all missionaries who were to get out before the turnover were advised to get out as soon as possible.

The next day, on August 20, I made arrangements with the telegraph-telephone office here to have a radio-telephone conversation with Eugene.

Communist Threatened Canton

When I was finally able to get through to Eugene above the static, the jangling of the operators, and possibly censors at either end, I gave him a condensed report of the situation. Hong Kong had been declared by the United States to be a part of the Atlantic Pact [the precursor of NATO] and therefore Communist attack upon that seaport would mean war with the United States. The

Communists had made many advances in China and were threatening Canton. Kunming would fall in six weeks or sooner.

British and American Missionaries—Lutherans, Baptists, and practically all of our own group here—were planning to leave because staying might cause the Chinese Christians trouble due to being associated with enemy aliens. Any work that might be done in Lisuland would probably not be a base-station proposition, and therefore all women, children, and families should probably evacuate as soon as possible.

When I first started talking with Eugene, he was still planning to try to go up-country. The lack of information at Likiang was manifest when Eugene asked, after my review of the news, "What is the Atlantic Pact?" At the end of the conversation, he said that he would wire me in several days about the entire group of missionaries coming out.

Chapter 2
Dysentery and Delays

Meanwhile, Mel Byers and I had been arranging for the Lutheran Plane to come to Kunming so that it could go to Likiang if needed. We had rounded up a load for the plane from Kunming to Hong Kong so that it would have a worthwhile payload returning to Hong Kong even if the Likiang flights did not turn out. We had worked days and days on the load, first for the 18th of August and then for the 24th. We had practically scoured the missionary population of Kunming, riding over bumpy cobblestone streets on bicycles to get that load.

On the evening of the day, I contacted Eugene, while I was working on further airplane arrangements, I became seriously sick with either dysentery or stomach flu, feeling really sick and weak, sometimes with acute pains in the abdomen. The next day the pains were sometimes very violent—a bad preparation for a crucial week ahead. I started taking sulphaguanidine, a total of 32 tablets within perhaps 18 hours. By Monday I was practically well, though somewhat weak.

Payload Arranged

Monday evening very late a telegram came from Eugene saying that all the Likiang missionaries wanted to come out as soon as a plane could be secured. The next day Mel Byers and I worked on getting a payload of Chinese to Likiang to cut down the total cost of the flights.

In the evening I contacted Eugene and made arrangements for a planeload of the missionary equipment and personnel at Likiang to be at the airfield the next afternoon, August 23, ready to evacuate. We needed to provide these details when requesting permission from the Communist authorities. Their permission would allow the missionaries to come out and allow the plane to land and take off without being seized.

Weather Problems and Communist Prison Fears

On the morning of the 24th, I received the necessary clearance message. Mel Byers and I waited and prepared all day for the plane to arrive from Hong Kong. When it finally came in about 4:30 p.m., after being delayed several hours in Canton because of a blown tire, it was too late to make any more flights. The next morning, the plane first

Dysentery and Delays

took a two-hour round-trip flight toward Chaotung up north to evacuate Methodist missionaries.

Mel Byers and I prepared our load to Likiang in the afternoon. About noon we found out that extremely stormy weather had forced the Lutheran Plane to turn back from Chaotung within 30 miles of its destination. We rushed to the airport to find the crew very much discouraged and not exactly willing to make a flight which might be communistically dangerous on top of the uncertain weather.

That morning I had made a radio-telephone call to Mr. Colley at Likiang. He had said it was cloudy but there were enough breaks in the clouds to see the ground for landing. And we did at least have the plane clearance telegram.

The weather problem was a comparatively minor one; mountains in this part of China are notorious, but the Red Star regimes of "liberation" are even more treacherous. One of the crew had spent about six months in a Communist prison once before and had no relish for repeating his experience. Both the engineer and the co-pilot—rugged and experienced fliers in the China area for years—argued that just several soldiers with tommy guns on the Likiang airstrip could hold up the plane once it had landed.

The American pilot, Bill Dudding, realized the dangers but wanted to evacuate the missionaries if at all possible. The entire group discussed, reasoned, and argued until well in the afternoon. When the case was put up to the Lutheran Mission director, he finally assented to the plane's making the try. It took off from Chennault field, over the mountains but beneath the clouds, about 1:53 p.m. Kunming time.

Pilot discussing the flight plan

Chapter 3

Flying Blind over Mountains—First Rescue

The two-engined craft warmed up its motors, thundered down the runway, and was in the air heading northwest about 1:57 p.m. Mel Byers and I were on board, ready to help out at Likiang. We passed low over the Kunming plain, near one end of the lake, and headed over the hills through a gap.

The cloud cover was fairly low, and since the pilot wanted to keep in sight of the ground as much as possible, he fairly skimmed over the white mountaintops. But after a short 10 minutes, he had to head into the thick clouds. On and on the plane roared through the milky white formations, flying blind. After perhaps 40 minutes of dense clouds, the pilot said in about three more minutes if he did not see any of the ground below, he would have to turn back to Kunming, for the plane was nearing a large lake.

Cloud-rimmed mountains were roundabout, but just above the lake was the break. The pilot swung around, having gotten his bearings from the lake, and headed down below the clouds, lower and lower, until one could see the individual pine trees on the ridges below. Then he headed low up a valley leading from the lake. Clouds hugged the mountainsides on either side of the narrow valley a short way above the plane. The sky itself was hidden by the murky formations.

The pilot guided the craft right up the valley. One could see the caravan trails winding around the mountainside, and villages with their individual houses nestling on the slopes. One could practically see the windows in the houses, few as such are in native abodes. The rocky cliffs seemed uncomfortably close to the plane.

A Memory of Eight Years Earlier

The Lutheran Plane, a DC-3 named *St. Paul*, crossed a large river which turned out to be the Yangtze. It crossed more mountains and then came out above a broad, thickly populated valley. Flooded rice fields made the valley appear almost like a huge marsh. The engineer came back to me and asked if I had any idea where we were. From my memories of eight years ago, I thought we might have come out onto one of the plains near Likiang, but the present valley was too long to be one of those. We might be flying over the Chien Ch'uan Valley, as I remembered that area was very similar to the one over which we were flying.

The engineer called me forward to talk to the pilot. I sorely wished I had gone over the area by air previously, instead of only on a jolting caravan mule, and even that more recently than eight years ago. In addition, eight years since going over a region once is not the best of preparation for guiding an aircraft over China. When I pointed out on a map to the pilot where I thought we might be, he said we could not have gone that far west.

I then thought we must be heading up the Hoking Valley toward Likiang, though I had never traveled it personally. If that were the case, we should shortly come to a low ridge or pass at the head of the valley separating it from the Likiang plain. Sure enough, in just a few moments we saw, off the nose of the DC-3, a range of low hills with a caravan trail heading over it, and a plain beyond. Then we saw the familiar outlines of a low hill in the plain with the city of Likiang nestling around it. We skimmed along the fields, just above the individual stalks of corn.

I told the pilot as well as I could remember from a transit stay there in 1941 where the mission compound was. We buzzed low over the rooftops to the side of the hill. Then we sped on up a side valley to the airstrip about 10 miles away from Likiang at the foot of a 21,000-ft snow peak.

The overcast was low, but we were still below it and could see the landing area up ahead. As we soared low over the pastures, horses and cattle went galloping, scurrying in fright across the fields. We circled the landing area in case the Communists had prepared a hot reception for us. We saw no machine guns or squads of soldiers, so the pilot lowered onto the well-worn strip on the grassy plain. As we rolled by, we saw a pile of baggage, a crowd of people, and Eugene waving to us on this 8,500-foot airstrip in the midst of Red-occupied China.

Relief and Joy

It was a relief not to be greeted by soldiers with Red Stars on their caps. However, when several of us on the plane started to take out cameras, Eugene and Mr. Butcher hurriedly told us to keep all such out of sight. Soldiers might appear at any moment and would be likely to confiscate such. Meanwhile, a mass of unruly peasants practically had to be fought off from boarding the plane. They wanted to grab baggage from incoming Chinese passengers in order to get paid for carrying them to Likiang. We started rushing the missionary baggage from the pile on the strip into the iron bird. Meanwhile, it was good to see Eugene again for the first time since saying goodbye last fall on the Union Station platform in Los Angeles, and to see Helen and the baby all doing very well except for nervous strain.

Speaking Lisu Once Again

I got to speak Lisu to Jesse, one of the Christians who had come down from the Salween Valley to accompany Eugene and Helen to the mission field. It was the first opportunity in six years for me to speak the Lisu language to a Lisu, but it was almost like old times and certainly a heartwarming experience.

While Mel Byers and the others took charge of loading the plane, I made some plans with Eugene. We made arrangements—together with the pilot Bill Dudding—for the remaining two or three flights to come in that Saturday and Sunday, August 27 and 28, to take out the rest of the missionary personnel and equipment at Likiang. Eugene and the Colley family would stay for the last flights. We almost didn't convince Helen with five-and-a-half-month-old David to come out ahead of Eugene, but finally did so.

Gold Dust

While Eugene and I were talking, he quietly motioned me aside from the crowd and slipped me a small, heavy, and very compact package. We were under observation by Chinese so this had to be done very quickly and unnoticeably. The package contained the equivalent of about 3,000 in Yunnan silver dollars (U.S. $750) in the form of gold dust which he had exchanged for his silver money intended for the work up-country, in order to keep from having it confiscated by the hammer and sickle. I took good care of the little package all the way into Kunming.

The plane was loaded and ready to take off within 20 minutes after landing. The ones going waved goodbye to those staying, the plane roared off down the runway, and soon was airborne. On the way back to Kunming, we flew high above the mountains instead of through the valleys below. This time, at least, we didn't have to worry about coming down through the clouds without radio guidance among unseen mountains. As the Butcher family and Helen with David landed at Chennault Field amidst the welcome party, the sun was shining very brightly over the Kunming plain.

Truck Problems

We were glad to get at least the first load out from Likiang. While everyone went home to recuperate and get reacquainted, Mel and I worked to have the planeload of baggage cleared through China's internal customs. After the customs officials had roundly "told off" the plane's crew for flying to Likiang supposedly without permission, the entire truckload of baggage was cleared, and we headed downtown.

Flying Blind over Mountains—First Rescue

The loaded truck

Mel drove the truck—a heroic and a marvelous achievement considering its nearly dead motor. And then, on the way into town the truck ran out of gas. So, the car accompanying us returned to the plane to get some aviation fuel for us.

Once the car left us to fend for ourselves, the truck stalled and had to be cranked vigorously to get started. I tried my hand at cranking, but Mel seemed to be the most successful. We finally got the truck down a narrow alley to deliver the Butchers' baggage.

When we started for Shang Hsipa, the truck once again wouldn't start. We cranked and pushed for about an hour and a half to try to get the heavy truck started. Half a dozen coolies and a crowd of bystanders helped, but the motor refused to start. Finally, I got a rickshaw to take me to borrow a jeep from a missionary across town. When I finally got back with the missionary and his jeep, the truck was gone; I found it back at the mission compound from which we had borrowed it. Mel and I left the baggage on the truck that night and returned home very tired at about 10:00 p.m. What a full day.

Chapter 4

Tommy Guns and Confiscations— Second Rescue

On Sunday, August 28, the crew and those other of us going up on the plane were to meet at 7:30 a.m. in front of the Central Air Transport Corporation hostel. Meanwhile, some more Chinese contacted me to go as passengers to Likiang. So before 7:30 a.m., Daddy helped in weighing in the passengers and luggage while I hurried on my bicycle to arrange airport transportation for the new passengers. Daddy then took over the weighing in and receiving payment of the passengers for the last flight later in the day; Mel Byers took care of getting a truck to take passengers to and from the field for the second flight; and I went on the plane to help at the Likiang airfield.

Loading the plane

Flying Over the Burma Road

The weather was not so good this morning, but there were plenty of breaks in the cloud formations to avoid flying low up the narrow valley as on the first trip. It was certainly refreshing to look down upon the mountains, valleys, and rivers winding in various directions.

Sometimes it was possible to see the Burma Road or some auxiliary motor road winding around the steep mountainsides below. It truly seemed marvelous to cross an area in only a few minutes that would take hours by car or, even tens of days by the age-old method of transportation in Yunnan: the mule.

Occasionally, one could see far below in the mountains a beautiful waterfall, though it would be out of sight before the camera could be readied. In time, the lake by which we had got our bearings several days ago came into sight, and after it, the mighty Yangtze zigzagging back and forth like a snake within the precipitous-sided gorge. Then we were above the Hoking plain again, speeding above the flooded rice fields. The next plain was our destination. In a few minutes, we had turned into the side valley and landed on the grassy landing strip.

Guns and Pistols

The air was more tense as we landed this time. We found that Communist soldiers had come the night before to the group waiting on the field—Eugene and the Colley family with their three children—to search their boxes and supplies. The "liberation regime" had already pasted paper seals across the lids of a large proportion of their boxes to indicate they had been inspected and the useful items confiscated. However, these avaricious soldiers, with practically uncontrolled power in their hands, wanted to see and "confiscate" even more of the white man's goods.

When we landed, there were no soldiers on the field; they were staying in a village about two miles away. As fast as we were able, we rushed the boxes and bundles onto the plane, hoping to take off before the soldiers arrived. As Eugene was loading a large drum, blue-uniformed soldiers came racing across the plain with their guns and pistols. They seemed breathless and a little peeved that we had come in their absence. They made us haul off the drum. Argument was useless. They looked over all the boxes to see if any without seals (or with broken seals) were on the plane.

Youngsters possibly 16 years old were carrying tommy guns. One unkempt soldier of the Red Star caps was apparently unfamiliar with guns and roved through the gathered crowd with his weapon sloppily pointed at person-level. We did ask him to keep his gun pointed in the air.

Finally, the plane was loaded. The head soldier checked the pieces of baggage. Then he asked me to lead him through the plane, pulling out his pistol and calling several more soldiers to follow him. He asked if anyone on the plane were carrying any guns; the answer was no. I led him and his associates forward through the inner door into the control compartment, asking them not to touch any of the delicate instruments. They peered into the various crannies and cubbyholes, apparently halfway expecting to see armed soldiers or stacks of machine guns there.

Finally satisfied, they retreated outside the airplane. Mrs. Colley and the children boarded the craft while Mr. Colley and Eugene waited for the next and last flight. The entire group of missionaries seemed extremely nervous and very glad at the prospect of getting out before being subjected to any more searches and "confiscations." For the second time in its Operation Rescue at Likiang behind the Communist lines, the Lutheran Plane roared off down the field and headed towards Kunming.

Chapter 5

Red Star Caps — Third Rescue

The sun was shining as the *St. Paul* took off for Likiang on its final run of Operation Rescue. I was in charge of the boarding of the plane and seeing that loading and unloading, especially at Likiang, was done as quickly as possible. In the flight manifestos for the Kunming airport control, Max, the co-pilot, listed me as "engineer."

On this flight, with good weather conditions, I was able to take a number of pictures on special infrared film. This kind of film is especially good for distant landscapes.

On this last flight, the general tension increased. Some of the Chinese passengers going up were very likely going to join the Communists at Likiang, but of course, it was not our business to question them.

I was somewhat concerned that the Likiang Red Star soldiers, should they find out that this was to be our last flight, would think the time opportune for seizing the plane for whatever little use they might be able to make of it, as scrap metal or otherwise. Of course, the other times they knew we were coming back, with passengers bearing merchandise to replenish their stocks.

As the plane rolled onto the landing strip at Likiang and came to a stop, a large crowd of natives awaited our arrival. A few soldiers stood in front of the crowd with their guns poised at us. As the doors of the plane were opened, the Chinese passengers climbed out and the soldiers crowded around. We weren't exactly sure for a moment what was going to happen. But then, instead of being violent, they seemed more friendly this time than before. We tried to cultivate their good feelings by asking them to keep the crowd of peasants from mobbing onto the plane.

Liberation Caps

We soon found out that, for some reason, they were expecting us to come back one last time in about three or four days. We did not contradict them. Quickly we loaded all the remaining baggage on the airfield into the plane. Then we asked the soldiers permission to take some pictures, hoping within our hearts they would not confiscate our cameras. They said we could do so, of anything other than the group of soldiers.

The pilot, Bill Dudding, and I tried to bargain with several of the soldiers for one of their blue "liberation" caps with the Red Star insignia. The head of the soldiers said that the caps were "government issue" and therefore could not be sold. However, he said, when we came back next time, he would have two such caps ready for us as a special gift. We accepted his offer.

All in all, we found the soldiers quite friendly on the surface, even willing to laugh with us. This was in spite of their searches and confiscations on the ground shortly before our arrival. Once again, the head soldier asked me to lead him and several other soldiers through the plane. Besides looking through the cubbyholes, this time they also looked through the personal suitcases of the crew. They begged our pardon for the trouble and retired to the outside.

50 Silver Dollars

For the last planeload, we had some extra room; consequently, Mr. Colley and Eugene had allowed two Chinese with two children to come aboard to evacuate. They seemed to be fearing for their lives, perhaps being on the Communist blacklist. Before permitting them to board, though, the soldiers found possibly 50 Yunnan silver dollars (about U.S. $14) which the woman was intending to use for future livelihood and perhaps also for her plane fare.

One of the soldiers came running with the silver to the head soldier, who was still guarding the door of the plane. We thought he was going to hand it to the woman, but then he hesitated and said that perhaps she had more silver than she needed. He proceeded to count out the silver to give the woman perhaps a third of it and keep the rest himself. The woman begged and pleaded, but to no avail.

We argued that the woman needed the money for the plane fare. He said she could sell her gold ring to pay for her transportation. We replied that it would not be enough. He was still resistant. Then I said, "Oh well, go ahead and give the money to the woman. We are all friends together, anyway." His fingers reluctantly let go of the money, but his action was a revealing example of the true Communist spirit under the polish of temporary non-aggression.

By this time, the motors of the huge iron bird had started warming up. With all the baggage and with the last of the white people in Likiang area—Eugene and Mr. Colley—aboard the plane, the Red Star soldiers may have had some misgivings as to whether the plane was really coming back in a few days. However, I reminded the soldier head about our agreement for the two Red Star caps, and he said, "sure thing," or the equivalent of it. The last of the soldiers got out, the door was closed, and the plane started taxiing.

Relief and Rescue Completed

The iron bird roared down the runway and climbed steadily up until it was over the fateful city of Likiang, which had not until now been left to the hands of the Iron Rule without the toning-down presence of the missionaries. The pilot climbed, passed an ancient temple on the hilltop to enable taking a picture of it, and then nosed over a mountain range and above the awesome abyss of the Yangtze Valley. From there it continued over the endless mountains of southwest China, the pilot occasionally veering the plane around a thundercloud amidst the blue sky.

Meanwhile, in the cubbyhole desk at the back of the cockpit, Mr. Colley and Eugene were fed cans of American fruit by the engineer as they expressed their relief and recounted some of their last experiences behind the Iron Curtain. I had some of the fruit too, since I had had time neither to eat breakfast nor lunch in the busy and tense work of Operation Rescue.

An hour and 20 minutes later, the sun shone especially brightly as the *St. Paul* lowered its landing gear and its flaps above the Kunming plain and nosed down to the capacious runway of Chennault Field. The plane even seemed a little proud of itself as it roared slowly to a stop beside the Customs House and stopped. A large group of missionaries was there to congratulate our completion of Operation Rescue. Even the Customs officials seemed a little more lenient, only opening a drum with clothes packed inside.

I wonder if the Communists up at Likiang are still wondering when the plane will come back. Although I'd sure like to get a Red Star cap as a souvenir from the trip, perhaps it would not be worth a special flight just for that.

Chapter 6

The Rest of the Story—Tighter Than a Drum

Letter No. 1

> 340 Shang Hsipa, Kunming, Yunnan, China
>
> September 2, 1949
>
> Dear Grandma, Aunt Louise, Aunt Eva, Ruth Margaret, and All:
>
> We are now, as reported by the world radio broadcasts, in Communist China. Or perhaps it would be more correct to say that we are no more in China since Yunnan has seceded from the Union. Reportedly, about two nights ago at 3:00 a.m., the C.A.T. [Civil Air Transport], General Chennault's

pro-Nationalist airline, received a secret but definite warning. That same morning, the women and children of the C.A.T. personnel were evacuated. They preferred the war-threatened city of Canton, about 120 miles from advancing Communist armies, to the semi-pacific city of Kunming.

The following night, though some weeks ago it was practically unheard of to have airplanes maneuver to or from the Kunming airport at night, members of the family here could hardly sleep a wink because of the roaring of airplanes all through the black hours of night. The next morning, we heard that practically all the operating personnel of C.A.T. had also removed themselves in the night.

One of the warnings of the consulate here in times past was that transportation—of which the main practical one is air—might be discontinued without warning in case of Communist threats, and that then it might be practically impossible to get out even before the Red armies come. This morning we heard the news (or was it yesterday morning?) that Yunnan Province had seceded from Nationalist China and that Kunming was in the hands of the hammer and sickle. We found also that the Nationalist 26th Army, which was several days ago encamped on the outskirts of Kunming and was depended upon to stabilize the city, moved out possibly yesterday or last night.

C.N.A.C. Flights Discontinued

Mel Byers and I were thinking of going to Chengtu in Szechuan Province en route to Batang and then to the mission field by way of Inner Tibet if we could somehow forge our way through. This morning we found that the direct air service to Chengtu had been discontinued. We proceeded to C.N.A.C. office to see if we could go by way of Chungking to Chengtu on its routing, only to find out that China National Aviation Corporation has suddenly canceled all domestic flights. It still is supposed to fly to Hong Kong and Rangoon, though. In a few days the domestic flights may be resumed, or else perhaps all service by air will be cut off.

Meanwhile, in the city, a strict curfew from midnight to 6:00 a.m. has been called. Martial law is supposedly in effect. We have been warned not to be out of our mission grounds or compounds after dark because of possible robberies and anarchy beyond the control of the local government. Yet the municipal police are guarding the streets heavily. Everyone is very tense and expects anything can happen within the next several days. We have tried to rush up evacuation of women and children and families. By the end of this week, practically none of the mission groups may still be in Kunming.

Letter No. 2

September 6, 1949

This morning the general situation has developed further in a negative sense. Sandbags are reportedly being put up on some of the streets.

We saw the Callaways off; they headed to the C.N.A.C. to check in at noon to fly to Hong Kong. Then I went downtown also to make arrangements about the Lutheran Plane and its further flights. In a short while, I found that practically all air service has been suspended.

I learned that the Callaways' C.N.A.C. plane to Hong Kong has canceled its Kunming stop and is to bypass Yunnan altogether.

Even the Lutheran Plane due today about 2:00 p.m. to evacuate some missionaries had trouble getting here. First, the plane radioed Kunming air control that it was going on a full itinerary elsewhere, and *possibly* Kunming, if permission were granted by the Hong Kong authorities. (Kunming is supposedly in Communist control, even though we see no Red Star helmets on the street yet.) But, after the Lutheran Plane had left Hong Kong, it radioed here that it was coming and to have all missionaries and baggage on the airfield.

They may have taken off officially for elsewhere and then decided to come here after they were in the air. The situation being as it is, we all need to pray that either the C.N.A.C. will make one or two more flights, or that the Lutheran Plane will be able to come several times yet. It looks as though the situation is getting tighter than a drum so far as getting out is concerned.

Now the question is the local situation. Pray for all of us. As to Robert and Betty and the others up-country [Isabel Dittemore and daughter Janet; David and Lois Rees with sons Emrys and Warren; Anzie Morse; Jane Kinnett; and Dorthy Sterling and son Markie], they may or may not be in a situation less disturbed than Likiang's and Kunming's. We are praying for them earnestly. Perhaps they will find it possible to evacuate through Burma, as indications are that they may have started to do so about the middle of August. They would have to travel a terribly difficult trail over an 11,000-foot pass. This would be the same route taken in 1944 when Dad, Eugene, and Robert rescued downed airmen.

Mel Byers and I, meanwhile, are considering and working hard on the possibility of going to Chengtu, Szechwan Province, and from there to Batang to try to reach the mission area from the north through Inner Tibet. The plan may or may not work out. Anything could happen these days.

With love to each one of you, yours,

R. LaVerne Morse

Letter No. 3

Kunming, Yunnan Province, China

September 7, 1949

There is at least a temporary lull now in the Communistic trends of Kunming, especially with the Governor Lu's going to Chungking to become conciliated to the Nationalist Government. Yesterday when the Lutheran Plane sailed down here to Chennault Field to evacuate a load of missionaries and equipment, the crew hardly knew what to expect.

The Hong Kong papers had apparently headlined premature news that Kunming, the capital of Yunnan Province, had fallen into the hands of Communists. Practically all the airlines had consequently stopped service into here. The only planes coming in and taking off from the extensive airport here yesterday were the Lutheran Plane and a C.N.A.C. cargo plane.

When the *St. Paul*'s crew heard that there had not been even fighting in the streets yet, they were considerably relieved. They are due back here day after tomorrow (Friday, September 9) to take out another load of missionaries, including some of our equipment and that of the Callaways. They will come again the next day, and then twice or three times a week. By that time practically all the missionaries who expect to leave Yunnan should be evacuated.

Lora Banks left about August 28 for the States by way of Rangoon. Imogene Williams left last Friday, September 2, for the missionary medical school in London. After getting down to the air office of the China National Aviation Corporation yesterday morning to go to Hong Kong and then finding that the flight had been canceled, the Callaway family this morning, at last, took off on the resumed flight. China will be a country almost barren of missionaries before long, it seems.

May God richly bless each one of you and continually enrich your lives with His Spirit and the Spirit of Jesus Christ.

Yours in the Service of our Lord Jesus Christ,

R. LaVerne Morse

PART III
Westward Toward Tibet

The decision is made to take the long way to Northern Burma. "Beautiful towering rock piers on the crossing places showed where once bridges once spanned the gorges. However, the original timbers had rotted. The bridge consisted only of swaying bamboo cables with a single row of boards laid on the bottom. Wild animals were plentiful. We saw monkeys and deer, and we heard leopards. On the seventh day we crossed a 10,900-foot pass into another major valley."

Chapter 1

Recognition Granted and Plans Made

*E*vents have been occurring in a way that I had never dreamed of before. The time spent in Kunming was very definitely useful. Besides getting Eugene and Helen out of a trap, I was able to work with my father on recognition of the mission by the Burmese government and their permission for the mission work to continue among the 35 or more Tibetan Lisuland Churches of Christ in the rapidly growing Burma area.

Though prospects for recognition and permission did not seem very good a month ago, I learned that our negotiations had been fruitful. A telegram awaited me here at the China Inland Mission from my father in Kunming: "Burma recognition granted."

The primary goal has been getting into the mission area before the Communists cut everything off altogether. If one could get into some of the more remote and inaccessible areas of the mission area, such as the border areas of Burma and Tibet, perhaps Dad could work for several years even though the Communists did take over all the surrounding governments. Working near a congregation in one of the most isolated jungle areas, perhaps one could train the leaders of the churches in that area.

There are churches in the established mission work, in distant jungles on the borders of Burma and Tibet, that have never yet seen the white missionary. There is one particular place I know of only through a hand-drawn map my brother Robert made several years ago. He had gathered details and exact locations of each congregation from the Lisu preachers who had led the work in those areas. If one could get through to such a place, he might be able to do invaluable good in strengthening the church during the time of crisis.

Such has been my hope during the past months. While I am thankful that at least parts of China have for now kept from falling to the hammer and sickle, it has appeared almost certain that the entire area will eventually go in the hands of the anti-religious, anti-Christian Communists. Whereas the original plan of going directly to the field by way of Likiang was first delayed and then made impossible altogether, we know that "all things work together for good to them that love the Lord." Perhaps the change of plans will work things more completely for the winning of souls in the future out here and that Tibet also may be reached.

Partnership Established

In Kunming I had become acquainted with Mel Byers, a sincere and capable Christian, working in association with Harold Taylor, whose work is going on today as a testimony of the gospel which he preached. However, with the oncoming of the Communists, the Taylor family evacuated to Japan.

Mel Byers, who had spent one and a half years studying Chinese, was planning to go first to Japan and then possibly back to the States. However, I suggested to him, after heart-to-heart talks, that perhaps the two of us together could do a very effective service for Christ in the Tibetan Lisuland area. It is always better for two missionaries to work together if they are going to be isolated from the help and companionship of other missionaries. In consequence of our talks back in August, we formed a sort of partnership for a year and a half and perhaps more if things work out.

Problems—Finding a Way

After the blocking of the Likiang route, Mel Byers and I planned to go into northernmost Burma by way of Fort Hertz. The landing strip there had been a forward operations field during the war with Japan. Eugene, Robert, and I had flown from it to India in 1943. The field might have fallen into disrepair since the war, but the pilot of the

Lutheran Plane, a veteran of the "Hump" during the war days, assured us that he could inspect the field from the air first so as to avoid any deep ruts during landing.

One major problem was that we could not get permission from the Burmese government to land at Fort Hertz. Since the mission had not yet been recognized by the Union of Burma, Mel and I might have additional trouble from the officials at Fort Hertz. (When Burma was governed by the British, members of the mission had been able to enter the country without visa or permits.)

Then the fatal word came: the Lutheran Mission Authorities did not want to risk their plane on such an attempt. We were rather glum and downhearted, but we prayed that God's will might be done and that He would open a way according to his will.

As a last resort, I had partially formulated a plan—even before the Likiang route had definitely closed to us—to enter the mission area by a very roundabout way:

- From Kunming northward in China to Szechuan Province by plane: several hours.
- From Chengtu, capital of Szechwan, to Yaan, Sikang Province, by truck: two days.
- From Yaan to Kangting (Tatsienlu), capital of Sikang, by *hwa-gan* (sedan chair) or on foot: 10 days.
- From Kangting to Batang, across the mountains and plateaus of Chinese Tibet by horseback: 20 days.

- From Batang, one could proceed by either of several routes, provided they could be opened and negotiated with the Inner Tibetans, by horseback and then on foot to the destination somewhere on the Burma-Tibet borders: 40–60 days.

I had inquired into the possibilities for this long journey and stored the facts away just in case they were needed. After the blocking of the other routes, we decided upon this one. So far, God has opened each stage of the journey in a way we would not have dared to hope.

Preparing the Payload

We made preparations to charter the Lutheran Plane to fly the two and a half hours to Chengtu. Mel Byers and I, with the help of several Chinese-Tibetans who were planning to go as far as Batang with us, worked to obtain enough passengers and cargo to pay for passage to Chengtu. We put an advertisement in the local papers, and within several days we had enough for the full load from Kunming

Date Set

This being China, we expected our flight, scheduled for Monday, September 12, to acutally depart about a week later. This time we were lucky. After several days of the plane taking evacuees and cargo to Hong Kong instead, during which our perturbed passengers nagged us for information, our flight to Chengtu was definitely set for Thursday, September 15.

Mel and I had determined we wouldn't believe that we were getting to Chengtu until the plane took off with us in it. Even then, the plane would very likely circle around and land back at Kunming. We weren't taking anything for granted. But on Wednesday we hurried to finish the last-minute items such as checking out at police headquarters, settling accounts, and so forth.

Thursday morning came and we arose before it was light. Besides getting our own supplies for several years off to the airport, we had to see about our paying passengers and cargo for Chengtu. Last-minute items of plane accounts had to be explained and turned over to Eugene, since he would be in Kunming at least some days yet. Mel Byers and I had prepared a fairly concentrated array of necessities. We had clothes for extremes of arctic and tropic conditions, a few concentrated foodstuffs, fairly extensive outlay of vital medicines, currency in various forms, stationery, and literature. (When you do not expect to be able to get anything except rice, salt, tea, and a few other items for several years, and you have to cut down on weight, you must be strategic.)

Chapter 2

Stowaway at 6,400 Feet

Thursday morning, we were to check in passengers and cargo at 8:00 a.m. at a mission compound downtown. Our boxes were also to be there before 9:00 a.m., when we should start for the airport in the dilapidated truck we had borrowed.

The horse cart we had ordered to transport our baggage did not come until about 8:30. Consequently, Mel went ahead downtown to check in passengers while I came afterward with the luggage. I took advantage of the opportunity to take a last look around our room and say goodbye to everybody not going to the airport.

Shortly after 9:00 a.m. everything was assembled downtown. We had some trouble with one man who had come on our suggestion that we might have last-minute vacancy on the otherwise full plane. Though there wasn't any space, he begged and pleaded because he had apparently sold everything in Kunming to go back home to

Chengtu. However, our plane was definitely loaded and extra weight might be disastrous.

The truck, with luggage and passengers piled high, jolted down the cobblestoned Kunming streets for the airport. In about 20 minutes, we were at the airfield amidst customs officials, police inspectors, and airline agents, all requiring the necessary clearances.

The customs officer on duty was reportedly a Christian. He looked at several of the parcels and then passed us. Some of the passengers had difficulty with the police because they had not acquired permission from the central police department to leave the city. I also hurriedly made out a manifesto of the cargo, my typewriter and paper with carbons being handy.

The Stowaway

When the *St. Paul* rolled down the runway at Kunming for takeoff, with my father, mother, Eugene, and Helen waving goodbye, the group of us on the plane bowed our heads briefly to ask God's guidance and protection on the journey ahead.

As the plane roared down the runway to gain speed to get off the ground, we sensed that there was something wrong. Instead of getting into the air halfway down the runway as a DC-3 should on a B-29 airstrip, the iron bird raced along the ground almost to the end. It was not until it reached the grass line grown end of the runway that the

Lutheran Plane strainingly climbed into the air, and even then, it did so wavering.

We found out that in addition to the heavy load we had figured on, the plane had about 400 pounds of extra weight in the 6,400-feet-above-sea level atmosphere. Included in that weight was one stowaway, the Chinese man we met earlier who somehow had gotten past the police, custom inspectors, and crew. We did not worry once we were safely in the air, but certainly, we had narrowly escaped disaster.

The plane roared safely on its way over the mountains towards Chaotung, the one stop en route to Chengtu. When the engineer, Otto, found out about the stowaway, he decided to bring the poor fellow to task. Unless he paid about one and a half times the regular fare before we arrived at Chaotung, he would be kicked off the plane at that stop. The man evidently did not have that much on him. Soon across the mountains and hills around could be seen a plain, and on it, a large, walled city. The *St. Paul* buzzed low over the city and came down on a grassy field. The engineer put off our stowaway as soon as the doors were opened, and in a way so that the man knew he was expected to stay off.

Chapter 3

Chengtu—Roast Duck and Rickety Rickshaws

The sun was shining over Yunnan Province, but when we crossed the border of Szechwan Province, and especially when we came near to Chengtu, the weather became dull and cloudy. Some of the passengers became airsick in the bumpy weather and therefore could not enjoy the ride very thoroughly. Really, though, it's thrilling to be able to look out endlessly above a sea of clouds, to be droning far above the jagged mountain tops, rivers, and plains.

After about two hours of ride since Kunming, the plane was heading low over a plain which seemed to spread endlessly on all sides. A large river was meandering across the heavily populated expanse. The overcast was low, but the iron bird was soaring below it anyhow. Finally, about 2:50 p.m. we passed low over a big city.

Below us I saw the large, stone Marco Polo bridge spanning a river. In a few moments we had landed at a barren airstrip and were parked at the end. About the only constructions nearby were some shacks and a tent or two. We hurriedly unloaded the baggage onto the ground beneath the wing of the plane. Soon some military police and an inspector came up in a car. The latter had us open several boxes and a package, and then said the rest were all right.

It's a Small World

On the field I noticed a white man who looked strangely familiar. He had come out to meet the *St. Paul* with outgoing cargo. Upon introducing myself I found out that he had been a cabin-mate of mine on the U.S. troopship from Bombay, India, to San Pedro, California, when I went back to the States during the past war. I remember yet the stifling hot cabin when we twice crossed the equator, and the new experiences of seeing Australia and Pacific flying fish. How small this world sometimes can be!

Szechwanese Versus Yunnanese

The group of passengers with cargo managed to get a ride into town on the truck of this former acquaintance. Almost immediately when we came through the streets, we could notice the great differences between Szechwanese life and Yunnanese. The people dressed differently here, quite often with turbans. They seemed to be more industrious in Szechwan than in Yunnan. Methods of work seemed different.

Instead of seeing the Yunnan-style horse carts, we saw carts each hauled by about four men with straps around their shoulders attached to the vehicle. Instead of the comparatively dirty tea shops with wooden benches, here we saw thriving, teeming "restaurants" with bamboo lounging chairs for all classes of people. Hundreds of roast ducks were being sold at little stands beside the roads. Everywhere bustled the lightweight, rickety rickshaws. There seemed to be comparatively little modernization and Western influence on the architecture as in many sections of Kunming. Chengtu, though the capital of Szenchwan Province, seemed to be merely a sprawling, age-old and little-changed city of ancient China.

Lost Correspondence and Currency

We found welcome accommodation at the China Inland Mission. After so much happening in one day, we now realized that we had actually left Kunming and that we were on our long journey. After supper, though, to my dismay, I found that a small blue plastic handbag, waterproof and zippered, in which were my passport, bank drafts, travelers' checks, several ounces of gold for currency, U.S. greenbacks, and all my accounts and correspondence, was missing.

That handbag contained the nucleus of what I needed for the entire trip to Lisuland. I kept a careful eye on it almost all the time, but while making customs arrangements, I had told one of the accompanying Chinese-Tibetans to watch the parcels. There had been a large crowd of Chinese around the truck when it was being unloaded. Now the handbag and all its contents were gone. I'd like to have kicked myself for not being more careful.

By this time it was dark and this section of Chengtu had its electric lights turned out for the night. All I could borrow to look around the house amongst the baggage was a half-dead flashlight. I also had a terrific headache. Finally, after praying that surely the handbag might be recovered, I went to sleep.

I was awakened by terrific thunder and a downpour of rain. In the morning the C.I.M. yard was covered with a full 18 inches of rain. This added to the picture of disaster; I probably was more worried than I had been in several years. I guess I should have had more faith. Just as I was telephoning Dr. Crawford to ask whether the handbag had been left in his truck, a station wagon drew up outside and he himself waved from the wheel. He pointed to something in the back seat. It was the blue plastic handbag!

Silk Cloth, Red Wool Yarn, Pens, and Watches

In the United States, one travels to work; in China one works to travel. At first, we had hoped to get off from Chengtu two days after arrival on the next major section of the journey. This was two days' journey by truck to

Yaan (Yachow). However, because of the terrific rain the night of our arrival, reportedly a bridge or two farther on had been washed out. With these delays, we did not leave until the sixth day.

We found out that any U.S. dollars to be exchanged into local currency had to be done now. That involved haggling at money exchangers for a fair rate, and then taking precautions to safeguard our funds for the coming months.

If a person gets into the interior and runs out of local money, even though he may have traveler's checks and drafts, he's stuck. Banks are non-existent there. Furthermore, we found that in Tibetan country, sometimes even silver money is hard to use. So, we used part of the silver to buy the proper grades of bright red and white silk cloth, cotton thread, red wool yarn, a few pens, and half a dozen inexpensive watches.

Being in a strange city, we had to shop around a lot to get the right items at the best prices. Furthermore, the streets didn't have simple names such as Locust Avenue, so that even when we were told what street we should go to, we sometimes got mixed up. There were no street signs of course. Once we hired rickshaws; I gave the name of a street, and we started off. Going about a block away, the rickshaws turned into a street and went for a way. The puller stopped and asked, "Is this enough? We've gone the entire length of the street." I found out I had given the wrong Chinese street name. Such are some of the novelties of travel in China!

Chapter 4

Westward

Our next big problem was getting transportation from Chengtu to Yaan in Sikang Province. A rather decrepit motor road stretches from the one province to the other. If one travels with about 30 pounds of equipment only, he can go by a Chinese bus. If he has more equipment, he may go by bus and send his equipment by a so-called "transportation company" all the way to Kangting, but his baggage will not reach Kangting for about six weeks. An alternative is renting space on a truck or chartering one to Yann and then personally supervising and arranging for transportation thence to Kangting.

We chose the last of the methods. In Chengtu, we were very fortunate to meet at the China Inland Mission several Kangting missionaries who were even then returning to their station. They helped us considerably in buying the necessary trade items, and in advising us what to buy to get best results with the Tibetans. Also, they helped us to charter a truck to Yaan. Thus, we were able to start off from Chengtu westward for the Tibetan border on September 21, 1949.

1941 Dodge and "Yellow Fish"

The truck journey to Yaan was all in all very satisfactory, especially since the truck company supplied us with a fairly good Dodge of possibly 1941 vintage. A big problem was the many soldiers who tried to pile onto the truck, already loaded high with baggage and with our own group. These "hitchhikers," called the "yellow fish" (*ywang yuag*), may even stop a truck at the point of a gun and so load down the vehicle that it gets mired in the muddy and rutted road. If the truck gets stalled or breaks an axle, the soldiers get off, let the others try to get the truck running again, and then demand to get on again when the truck goes off.

We had persons posted on the running boards of the truck and at the corners in order to keep off the undesirables as much as possible. We were fairly successful until the truck stopped at a highway check point. Then, almost before we realized it, about a regiment of soldiers (so it seemed) start to swarm on. By arguing and a bit of shoving off, we managed to get part of them off but had to go ahead with about six of them. Later in the day, we got stuck in a big rut in the clay. After about two hours of trying to pry the truck out, finally the truck engineers at our suggestion dug the truck out.

We stayed the first night out of Chengtu at a dark, smelly Chinese inn in the city of Chong Lai. The next day as we neared Yaan we came to a roadblock where a group of Sikang provincial soldiers were examining all trucks, supposedly for opium and firearms. At the end of a long line of seven loaded trucks, we were met by the officer in charge, twirling a pistol on his finger with another pistol at his belt.

He was very insolent, apparently holding out for a bribe from us. We waited for a while trying to get through. We finally went back to a village behind us to see a higher officer. We contacted the division commander for the entire road, got a pass from him, went back, sharply reproved the formerly insolent officer, and roared on past the long line of trucks. After climbing a high mountain, we came down in a narrow valley to the city of Yaan (Yachow) where we were welcomed by Dr. and Mrs. Crook of the American Baptist Mission.

Friendly Help

At Yaan, because of the high cost of going to Kangting by hwa-gan (sedan chair), we decided to go by the much slower method of walking and having our equipment carried by coolies, even though we found their price rather high for our limited supply of silver money. Then we happened to visit a certain Colonel Fu of Batang who was in the city. He was very influential throughout the province and has in times past been very friendly to the missionaries.

Through him we were able to get carriers much more cheaply, and also to get notes of introduction to checkpoints along our route so that we would not be stopped further by soldiers. After three days at Yaan, we continued with 16 coolies for Kangting on September 25. By the way, though the coolies carried about 125 pounds apiece according to the rather inhuman Chinese custom, only about half of the total baggage belonged to Mel and me. The rest belonged to the four Tibetans with us and to Mr. Nichols, a missionary at Batang.

Chinese coolie

Chapter 5

Gorges, Rocky Cliffs, and Reader's Digest

The trip from Yaan to Kangting was an opportunity to see some of the most impressive scenery in the world. The river which we first followed descended through a continuous succession of gorges. Rocky cliffs 2,000 feet high towered up from the river. The coolies with their loads took about 10 hours to travel what we could walk in three. So, we would go ahead every few hours to take pictures, look at the scenery, drink Chinese tea, and read the *Reader's Digest* or the *Manual of Clinical Therapeutics*.

Gorges, Rocky Cliffs, and Reader's Digest

Yaan Sikang Pass

I learned a lot about diseases and medicines from the time spent in reading. I quickly found that China abounds with diseases of all sorts. Cases ranged from muscle soreness and sore eyes to malaria, bacillary dysentery and/or cholera, and possibly typhoid fever and tuberculosis. People in our group came to me for treatment in the evening when we had reached our day's destination. You can imagine that I felt rather inadequate. However, frequently referring to the medical book, I was able to make good use of the medicines. As many as 20 people in an evening would come for treatment, but I finally had to stop giving them out because they would be most needed later on in the Burma-Tibet area.

As we continued through the mountainous country, we learned that the road we followed had been a motor highway during the past war. It extended from southwest

China (Chengtu) north along the Tibetan border far to the northwest of China. Now, however, it had fallen into disrepair. Rockslides had occurred in places where the road had been blasted around tremendous cliffs.

Beautiful, towering rock piers on the crossing places showed where bridges once spanned the gorges. However, the original timbers had rotted and often the bridge consisted only of swaying bamboo cables with a single row of loose boards laid on the bottom.

Wild animals were plentiful as we continued toward a mountain pass. We saw monkeys, deer, and we heard leopards. About the seventh day out of Yaan, we crossed a 10,900-foot pass into another major valley, into which leads the valley of Kangting. Near the top of the pass during a few brief moments when the clouds parted, we sighted a mighty snow mountain, the 24,900-foot Minya Konka. The descent from the pass was very sharp and rapid. In consequence it was not until we arrived in Kangting that we recovered from a set of severely sore leg muscles and toe blisters.

Several times we went swimming in the icy cold streams. On the 10th and 11th days of the trip afoot from Yaan to Kangting, we followed up a valley. The stream dropped so rapidly that as we came the first 10 miles of the valley, we saw hardly a bit of green water. It was all milky white, a mass of foam churning amidst mighty boulders in what seemed a continuous series of waterfalls. Meanwhile, the rocky mountainsides arose precipitously on all sides and occasionally a snow-capped peak appeared in the dark blue sky above.

All in all, I do believe the scenery was more impressive that any I have seen in the States or Canada, perhaps including the Canadian Rockies.

Mel and I arrived in Kangting early the morning of the 11th day. The Tibetans arrived several hours later, and the carriers arrived about 4:00 p.m. We all stayed at the China Inland Mission, enjoyed the fellowship, and learned many things about working in Chinese Tibet.

A view before Kangting

PART IV
Plateau Journal

Traveling 59 days from Western China into Tibet in 1949 was an extremely dangerous venture. Thievery and banditry abounded. Passage through the land required nearly unattainable permissions from Tribal Rulers. An unexpected turn led LaVerne and Mel to get swept into a caravan led by one of Tibet's most powerful and influential leaders, Pangda Tsang, who was returning from a negotiation with the Chinese government to protect Tibet. "You can imagine our pleasurable surprise," wrote LaVerne, "to find out that he was the very same person who entertained, as special guests, my parents along with Eugene and Robert for a month or two at Gartok, Inner Tibet, about 25 years ago."

Chapter 1

Preparations and Good Fortune

Our 10 days in Kangting were very busily occupied preparing for the next stage of the journey. For one thing, all our equipment had to be packed in boxes not exceeding 80 pounds for carriage on Tibetan horses and yaks on the high plateau and on narrow mountain trails. The boxes then had to be sewn completely in yak skins to waterproof them in case we should ford deep streams en route. Because food would be practically unavailable on the desolate, high-altitude plateaus, we had to plan, buy, and pack food for 20 days for the six of us including the four accompanying Chinese-Tibetans.

Side street in Kangtang

Part of the route lay over mountains as high as 17,000 feet above sea level with plenty of snow in prospect. Consequently, we got out all our artic-weather clothing and then bought Tibetan woolen *chupas* as well—heavy, clumsy-looking garments about like a huge blanket with sleeves. Amidst business, though, on one day I climbed to Horse Race Mountain, a high shoulder above Kangting where the Tibetans annually hold rough-and-tumble races on their mountain-bred ponies.

Pangda Tsang

The day we arrived in Kangting, we met two young British missionaries who had been trying for about a year and a half to get across southeastern Tibet to India. Now they were at last getting started, with the help of a powerful and influential Tibetan caravan trader and chieftain reputed to have control over 80 percent of Tibet's commerce.

The following day, the two Britishers, George Patterson and Geoffrey Bull, introduced us to the Tibetan chief. You can imagine our pleasurable surprise to find out that he was the very same person, Pangda Tsang, whose special guests were my parents with Eugene and Robert for a month or two at Gartok, Inner Tibet, in 1925, about 25 years ago.

Pangda and his brother, Raga, were very much delighted to renew the family acquaintance. They asked about Robert and Eugene, even remembering their names, and remembered going hunting with my father, and also his preaching. Drinking Tibetan buttered tea in the Pangda Tsang residence, with his special guards around, we became acquainted with a number of Tibetan chiefs and reputed warriors. We found out that after having been in Kangting for several years, their families were planning to cross the high plateau lands of Sikang Province, Chinese Tibet, to the border of Inner Tibet near Batang.

Pangda made arrangements for us to go with him. The route being notorious for its bandits, travelers generally have to wait a month or more in Kangting for a sufficiently large and well-armed caravan to assemble. However, we spent only 10 days in Kangting, barely long enough to make all the preparations, before starting out with Pangda

Tsang's small army of Tibetans with swords, pistols, rifles, and machine guns.

Brightest Clothes and Fanciest Horses

After having been in Kangting for several years, Pangda Tsang was evacuating with all his Tibetan soldiers armed with swords and every sort of firearms possible, including machine guns. Besides Mel and me and the two Britishers, many other groups were taking advantage of Pangda's protection.

The tremendous procession that set out for Tibetan country on October 17 was undoubtedly the largest group to leave the town in months or perhaps years. Practically everyone of rank in the provincial capital, and all the friends of those in the caravan, were out to see the group off, everyone wearing his brightest clothes and riding his fanciest horse. There must have been as many as 150 horsemen. Truly, it was a picturesque and colorful sight. Even the horses seemed to catch the spirit of the party as they trotted past the gate of the town and up the trail westward.

Chapter 2

Pangda Caravan and Reader's Digest

The first day, we climbed upward toward the 14,500-foot pass that led to the 12,000-foot-high plateaus of Chinese Tibet. After stopping for the night, a group of us climbed up a hill to a hot spring, where we took open-air baths with the snow beginning to fall around us. We began to get acquainted with other members of the party, too.

LaVerne and Mel on the high plateau

Sunom, Raga's son and Pangda Tsang's nephew, had grown up to a large extent in Kalimpong, India. He had gone to an English-speaking school in India and later also to an American school in Nanking. Thus he really spoke school-boy English as well as Tibetan. Jigme, Pangda's son, having had his education in Kangting, knew no English but was well acquainted with Chinese. Raga, Sunom's father, though taking a secondary place in relation to his brother in rank with the Tibetans, was well acquainted with English. Day after day, while riding his magnificent mule, he would read copies of the *Reader's Digest* which we had brought along. Then he would discuss with us anything from politics to agriculture.

Middle-aged Pangda Tsang was the same sharp-eyed but jovial person who, in his younger days, had fought and won many a borderland fight. Almost every day we would have *tsamba*, [barley] flour for a dumpling-like concoction, and buttered tea with him, along with large chunks of boiled yak or goat meat from which each person would cut off mouthfuls with their knives. Thus, we found out the two important Tibetan implements for eating: fingers and knives.

Accordion and Chants

Besides some Chinese merchants and officials and the array of Pangda Tsang's warriors and servants, an interesting figure in the caravan was a Hindu priest from India. Somehow in his pilgrimages he had made his way to Kangting, and Pangda had become his patron. Night after night, with Mel playing his accordion on one side of the camp, the Indian lama would go through his ritual of ringing his bell and chanting in a rising and falling voice, "*Radesham, radesham; kita ram, kita ram.*" He was very sociable. We were able to have a number of talks on Christianity with him and with the members of Pangda's family and group. I also had several talks with Pangda about the possibilities of doing missionary work far within Inner Tibet. Perhaps someday this will bear fruit to the advancement of the gospel.

Pangda's soldiers

LaVerne in Tibetan clothing

Blue Sheep, Antelope, and Ptarmigans

Almost every day, groups from the caravan went hunting on the mountains or in the hills and forests. During a day's stopover at Yachung, a group of us went hunting for the famous blue sheep of this area. We spent an entire day around cliffs and precipitous slopes, Mel and I climbing possibly 5,000 feet. However, this time all we saw were some squirrels, a chipmunk, three huge pheasants, a flock of wild pigeons, and a rabbit, none of which we were able to shoot.

On another occasion we went up a grass-covered mountain from a camp at possibly 15,000 feet to the summit at perhaps 17,000 feet to hunt for antelope. In all these expeditions, it seems that the wild animals were too wily for the white man. Then, when I had a good opportunity to shoot something, my borrowed gun wouldn't fire. A number of Tibetans and I saw some ptarmigans from across a valley, so I borrowed a .30 carbine from Sunom and went after the birds.

Horses at the base of the mountain

Ptarmigans are large white birds, about the size of geese, with red faces (don't ask me why the blush), red feet, and black wingtips. Clambering over the mountainside until dusk without seeing the birds again, I tried to shoot some smaller birds, but the gun wouldn't go off. Then, as I climbed across a landslide, a Tibetan called to me that there were some ptarmigans near me. Apparently, his gun wouldn't go off either. I climbed over a knoll, and there within about 40 feet, nine beautiful ptarmigans, looking huge and resplendent in their colors, marched past me in single file. I pulled the trigger anyway, but the gun only clicked without striking the bullet hard enough to explode it. I picked up a rock and ran after them, but by then they were gone. I would have done better with a camera than a gun.

Anything but Hurried

Traveling in a caravan with Pangda Tsang turned out to be anything but hurried. Half a day's easy riding would be the extent of one day's travel. Getting up at dawn, the caravan would quickly eat breakfast and then set off. About three or four hours later, Pangda would call a halt for the day. Camp would be quickly set up and the loaded yaks and horses turned out for pasture. Thus, we had plentiful opportunity for hunting on the bare slopes or up some forested valley. Fallen pine needles, drying grass, and brilliantly clear autumn skies were truly perfect for camping and traveling. Of course, with the high altitude it was often freezing cold; but even so, we enjoyed swimming a number of times in the broad, clear streams.

Pangda's caravan camp

Cooking dinner

Only a few times did we see the huge, stone, fortress-like Tibetan houses which make up the very few habitations of much of the route. Several times, however, we saw nomad yak-herders' camps with their black yak-hair tents. While the route is notorious for bandits, we found that many of them were ardent followers of Pangda Tsang. Consequently, Pangda himself said the main danger would be that bandits might attack parts of the caravan, not knowing that it was his. Thus, on certain occasions he would send ahead scouts to head off robbers or to forewarn the caravan of any possible attack. One day we received the report that there were 30 bandits ahead, but upon entering the territory the following day we saw none.

Chapter 3

Litang—14,000 Feet

On November 1, we all looked forward to one great step in the journey, the arrival at Litang, Sikang Province, over half the way from Kangting to Batang. We had heard rumors that the place might be in Communist hands when we reached it—we of course had been out of contact with outside news for three weeks—but we found the rumors false.

About mid-morning, we were met by a band of armed horsemen all dressed in their best clothes. They were some of the leaders of Litang who, upon hearing that Pangda Tsang was coming, had come far out from town to meet his party. We all dismounted to regroup the party and then proceeded. Passing a sort of plain with a small hill, we came to the plain on which Litang is situated. As we neared the town, everyone started to trot his horse. About 25 or so horsemen, most of them armed, rugged Tibetans, rode faster and faster across the plain. All of a sudden, we were all galloping, at intervals being joined by additional people meeting us. It was fun! We galloped harder and harder across the plain until finally we swept amidst the dust into the Tibetan town of Litang.

Galloping across the plain

From Running to Exhaustion at 14,000 Feet

Its elevation of 14,000 feet makes the town of Litang one of the highest in the world. Though usually one of the least of my troubles is getting to sleep after a full day, at this altitude and its thin air, I found it difficult. Not only that, but any kind of exertion also left us exhausted within several minutes.

One day, in going to a feast which some of the leaders of the town were giving for Pangda Tsang and the four foreigners, I started out running to catch up with the rest of the party, which had gone ahead. Very soon, however, I slowed to a fast walk and then almost dragged along, exhausted.

Guests at the Fourth Largest Lamasery in Tibet

About two years ago, there was a terrific earthquake in Litang which killed 1,000 people. The lower part of the town even now consisted to a large extent of ruined houses, walls without any roofs.

One of the noted features of Litang was the large lamasery above the town. It was known as being the fourth largest in all Tibet, the three largest all being in Lhasa. About 4,000 monks were supposedly enrolled in this lamasery.

Lamasery in Litang

Litang—14,000 Feet

One day, we had the honor of being guests at the lamasery with Pangda Tsang and a high official of the Chinese government. We were taken through the various "sacred" parts of the place, including the most sacred part probably seen by few, if any, white people before. In one room was a huge *chorten* or shrine which was said to have 113 ounces of gold in decorations. In addition, the dishes for the butter offering were said to be of pure gold.

As guests of the treasurer of the monastery, we had a Tibetan feast. Very different from Chinese feasts, this one consisted largely of steamed bread and huge pieces of boiled meat. Each person took a huge joint of boiled yak meat and a dagger-like knife. Thereupon he cut off as much as he could chew at one time. At intervals, he would eat some bread or drink plentifully of Tibetan buttered tea.

After finishing the one feast at about 2:00 p.m., we were very much surprised that we had another feast to attend at 4:00 p.m. the same afternoon with a high Chinese official. Somehow, we failed to eat very much at the second feast that afternoon! During the four days we were at Litang, we went to five feasts. These feasts were a welcome change from the more restricted diet, namely of tsamba, which we had on the road.

George Paterson, Mel, lamas, and Pangda's men

The Birthplace of the Sixth Dalai Lama

Our housing in Litang was rather historical. The local people had arranged for Pangda Tsang and his party to stay in a large Tibetan-style house, where a large room with couches and tables had been prepared for us. Around us were hundreds of bales of Pangda Tsang's tea, part of his business into Tibet. Most interesting, though, was that the house was the birthplace of the sixth Dalai Lama of Lhasa. Accordingly, it was considered very sacred. The walls were covered with ornate, many-colored Lamaist paintings. Carvings and idol figures further "adorned" the place.

Mel liked to play his piano accordion, and the rest of us liked to listen. One time, though, when he had been playing the instrument vigorously, some of the local people came with a special request that the accordion not be played inside the building, because the idols upstairs were being disturbed. Thence Mel could play outdoors but refrained from doing so inside.

Yak Meat

Litang was noted for its yak-meat-drying business. Apparently, the town's high altitude and lack of insects with plentiful sunshine was ideally suited to the slaughtering of yaks. Large herds would be driven into Litang for sale. Of course, at the slaughtering places there were also large flocks of crows. A more impressive bird especially prominent at Litang was a huge golden eagle which could be seen every day flying about or solemnly perched on a hill overlooking the valley.

Chapter 4

A New Caravan and 60 Loaded Yaks

From Litang, Mel and I parted from the company of Pangda Tsang. He was headed toward a place south of Batang, and we needed to go directly to Batang, hoping to reach it in about seven days of travelling. We continued in the caravan of a highly reputable Chinese-Tibetan official of Batang, Liu Chia Chu, who had happened to work with Mrs. A. L. Shelton [the wife of Albert Shelton, J. Russell's mentor who brought the Morses to Tibet] in the early days of missionary work there. The rest of the journey to Batang was not quite so exciting as with Pangda Tsang, but we had a lot of fun anyway. This time our companions consisted largely of Chinese and Chinese-Tibetans.

The caravan consisted of possibly 60 loaded yaks and 20 riding horses. Yaks are peculiar animals—burly and lumbering, with long, black hair and a striking resemblance to American bison. They seem to have no vocal abilities except a surprising pig-like grunt. They look very clumsy, and yet seem to get along better on mountain trails with 160-pound loads on their backs than horses do. They thrive on high altitudes such as 15,000 feet above sea level but are likely to get sick and die when driven to such uncomfortably low altitudes as 8,000 feet!

Sixty yaks

Horseback at 15,000 Feet

We started out up a valley from Litang, seeing a few mountain goats on the mountainsides. When we arrived at the second day's camping place about 1:00 p.m., the owner of our group's horses insisted upon our going perhaps 15 miles farther to his nomad village, supposedly to get fresh horses. The region was notorious for robbers, and Mel and I with the accompanying four Chinese-Tibetans were skeptical of leaving the main caravan. However, the horseman assured us that there would be no danger of robbers so long as we were with him, for he knew and was one of the people. Thus, we tied our bedding rolls on the backs of our saddles and continued with him. We found our destination lay across an astounding plain about 15,000 feet above sea level, surrounded by high peaks and mountain ranges.

Sandhill Cranes and a Nomad Village

We trotted and galloped across a trail in the general direction of the nomad village. The horseman, a rugged, uncombed, unwashed Tibetan clad with a huge floppy sheepskin garment, led us up the plain and across a stream with its surrounding marshes toward a group of distant black dots at the base of a bordering mountain range.

We saw a number of huge sandhill cranes, flocks of the rare, golden-colored shell-drakes, and then herd after herd of antelope in the distance. The horseman explained to us that the local nomad inhabitants of the plain were not allowed by their *bembo* (official) or the lamas to kill the abundant wildlife around them. Apparently, the regulation is part of their religion. Later we came upon a big herd of yak, and various smaller herds of sheep and goats.

Nestled at the foot of the mountain range at the edge of the plain, near a half-frozen stream, was the nomad village. This consisted of black yak-hair tents, each with plenty of space around for tying up the yaks at night. That night we feasted on fresh meat, sour buttermilk curd with brown sugar (this is quite delicious), buttered tea, and milk. In a way, we envied the rugged but nevertheless apparently healthful life of the Tibetan nomads.

Campsite cooking

An accompanying traveler

Mel Byers

Tent Villages

The following day, we had a long trip across the plain in another direction to catch up to the main caravan. Our accompanying horsemen explained to us that it takes eight days' travel to go around the plain. There seemed to be nomad villages all around it, though, with an estimated half million head of yak being herded in by the inhabitants. With the tent villages were also camps of lamas in arrangements like monasteries—10 or 20 white tents with one central, large tent for the ceremonies.

A Frantic Herd of Antelope

We found abundant herds of antelope—hundreds of antelopes—all over the plain. As we approached the other side of the plain, we were going up a sort of grassy valley. Possibly 60 antelope were up-valley from us and showed unrest at our approach. Riding good horses, we fanned out across the valley, with Mel Byers nearest the left-hand mountain.

All of a sudden, a Tibetan appeared over the knoll at the head of the valley and headed toward us on the far side of the antelope herd. The latter started running and then racing frantically from side to side. Finally, the entire herd headed along the base of the left-hand mountain down the valley. Mel's horse caught the spirit of the occasion and responded by galloping toward the mountain. But the herd continued to pour onward. Mel rode right into the onpouring herd and could practically have caught an antelope with his hands. I followed close after and came within 40 feet before the herd completed racing by. Well, it was fun, even if we didn't have guns to collect a permanent souvenir of our experience.

Photos Only

The next day, having caught up with the main caravan, Mel and I borrowed several heavy rifles. The caravan was taking a day off from travelling, so we came back toward the plain and had an exciting day of stalking the antelope. We got some wonderful sights of the beautiful, curving-horned creatures, sometimes very close, but the only acquisition was on my camera. The guns weren't worth two bits; the bullets sometimes wouldn't fire, and we were punk shots. We must have been awfully punk shots or else the gunsights awfully inaccurate for us to miss at 50 feet! The picture I got on my camera was of an innocent antelope that wouldn't run away after I had missed my last bullet at it. Well, it was fun, anyway.

Tibetan Tea

After the fifth day of travel from Litang, the group of horse-riders packed foodstuffs and bedding on the horses and forged ahead of the slower yak caravan. We had quantities of boiled yak meat, *go kwei* (round, hard, half-inch-thick bread), tsamba, tea, and Tibetan butter. The latter, being always in varying degrees of rancidity, is an ingredient combining the qualities of butter and blue, mold-streaked Roquefort cheese. However, churned in tea with sufficient salt, it makes the necessity of the Tibetan road: buttered tea.

Ice-and-Snow-Made Lakes

We had crossed over one pass at perhaps 16,000 feet and then climbed for the highest point of the entire route, a pass estimated at about 17,000 feet. As we approached this last pass, we entered an awe-inspiring, gorgeous, glaciated canyon. Rock cliffs and peaks rose thousands of feet into the sky, formations near the summits like idols on a pagoda with occasional caves deep into the cliffs. The cirques or glacier-made amphitheaters could be seen high up in the mountain range. As we climbed toward the pass, we saw two huge rock peaks rising hundreds of feet like pillars into the blue sky. Below the pass were a number of ice-and-snow-made lakes. Finally, we were atop the pass. Much of the world in sight was below us off in the distance. And yet, on almost every side were yet higher mountains and peaks.

We descended into the valley that leads to Batang and camped after sundown that night a short way below the tree line with fir and cedars around us. That night, there was a feeling of excitement in the air as we anticipated our arrival at Batang, Sikang Province, on the border of Inner Tibet, on the 59th day of our journey from Kunming.

Chapter 5

Batang Apples, Chinese Cookies, and Walnuts

The next morning, we descended sharply through magnificent fir and cedar forests. Then we noticed signs of cultivation, the first in many days of travel across the highlands. We came to a lone, flat-topped Tibetan house on the mountainside, and a group of Batang Tibetans welcomed the party with the famed Batang apples, Chinese cookies, and Tibetan buttered tea. We stopped to partake of these refreshments.

Further down the trail, I noticed an unusual and rare specimen of life: another white man. He was Ellis Back. Shortly after, I met Edgar Nichols, head of the other missionary family at Batang. They had ridden up the trail to meet us. They took Mel and me to another welcoming party in a Tibetan house near the road. We ate more apples, walnuts, and muffins, and drank more buttered tea. We had an enjoyable time of visiting and catching up on the latest news as we continued down the canyon on the dusty trail.

Magistrate, Provincial Officials, and Military Commanders

Half an hour's journey outside of Batang, we stopped a third time as we were welcomed by Chinese officials and leaders of the province. They had come out largely to meet the Chinese Nationalist representative, Liu Chia Chu, who had come out this far with us. Mel and I again stopped to eat apples, walnuts, muffins, and sunflower seeds, and to drink buttered tea with Ellis Back and Edgar Nichols and their families. The magistrates and the military commander of Batang came over to greet us, on account of Liu Chia Chu. After a short time of visiting and lunching, our group continued down the valley and in a short while came in sight of the Batang lamasery, the Batang valley, the town of Batang with its Tibetan-style flat-top roofs and red-mud houses, and then the missionary grounds on the nearby hill. We entered the town gate of Batang at 3:27 p.m. on Saturday, November 12, 1949.

Trotting and Galloping

One of the great pleasures of the trip was riding good horses. Tibetans like to ride, and some of their horses can really go, trotting or galloping. My favorite horse was a fiery, wild black one I rode from Litang to Batang. When it was first being saddled in Litang, it broke both the tailpiece and the reins. When I did manage to get on it, it went racing across the plain, and I had to hold on with all my effort to keep from being thrown off. It would shy at the slightest pretense so that I soon learned to avoid giving it the slightest excuse. Even so, several times it bolted and tried to throw me. I liked it though, because I could get it to go racing down the trail about anytime I wanted.

Batang at 9,000 Feet

Batang was a town of about 2,000 population. This consisted partly of Tibetans, partly of Chinese, and a large proportion of Chinese-Tibetans. The place was a sort of last outpost of the truly Chinese government on the border of Inner Tibet in Sikang Province. Located in a valley about a mile and a half wide and surrounded by high mountains, it was noted for its moderate-all-year weather even though it is about 9,000 feet above sea level. However, during our stay there we began noticing the first clouds in about a month of perfect weather.

Batang

Batang is especially noted for its delicious American varieties of apples grown all over the valley. The first trees were started 30 years ago by the missionaries who were withdrawn under the U.C.M.S. in the late 1920s or early '30s. At any rate, apples were a part of the daily consumption; Mel and I were glad to take advantage of our opportunity. Moreover, though not modern to the extent of having any electric lights, Batang did have telegraphic connection with the outside world through a government radio transmitter which ran on batteries. Hence, I was able to communicate with my father in Kunming.

A Homecoming of Sorts

Ever since the day before Mel and I arrived in Kangting across the province, we had been meeting former acquaintances of my parents. But here in Batang, practically everyone remembered the time when my parents were there about 24 years ago, before they started out as direct-support missionaries. Of course, since that time all of the U.C.M.S. work has closed down. The missionaries at Batang now, the Nichols family and the Back family, are directly supported by New Testament Churches of Christ in America. However, when I walked down the streets, I was welcomed almost every time by someone who remembered—and cherished—the *Mo Mu-si* (Missionary Morse) and family who used to run the evangelistic section of the former "organizational" mission work.

Many of the present leaders used to have my father as their teacher a quarter century ago. One elderly, likable Tibetan greeted me on the street with a beaming face; he used to be one of my parents' personal helpers many years ago.

The pastor of the present congregation explained to me about the chapel building which was again in good use: its construction was directed by J. Russell Morse. When Mel and I were invited to several Chinese feasts for the travelers of the incoming caravan, we met additional people who had known my parents well many years ago. Thus, coming to Batang was very much like a renewal of old acquaintances of the family.

The Political Situation

When we left Kangting, the missionaries there had expected that place to turn Communist within a month. Before we arrived in Litang, rumors had us halfway fearful we would find it Communist when we arrived. We were certainly glad to find out that Batang had not yet turned, but it nevertheless seemed to be a very uncertain place. A large element in it, especially the students, seemed to be Communist or pro-Communist. There was very serious talk of the town and the surrounding area shifting allegiance from the Nationalist Government in the very near future.

. . .

[Editorial note: Meanwhile, the Morse family in Kunming had been delayed in leaving, waiting for permits from the Burmese government to work in that country. The political situation became increasingly tense. On November 24, Eugene, Helen, and Drema Esther flew to Hong Kong. The situation continued to deteriorate, and Russell insisted that Gertrude go on and join the family in Hong Kong. She left December 7, and on December 9, 1949, the Communist takeover was complete, leaving J. Russell no way out. It would be two and a half years before he would reunite with the family.]

PART V
Tibetan Journal

LaVerne and Mel journey from Batang to the Salween Valley, across "Forbidden Tibet." First, they are held as prisoners, and then they are escorted as honored guests. They travel through frozen lands unknown to the outside world. "Life at a Tibetan fortress at a 10,000-foot altitude amidst the cold plateaus and mountains of the borderland must be like a page or chapter out of *Beau Geste*.... Early in the morning, we were awakened by the sound of lama horns, flutes, and drums. Then there was a terrific boom of a mountain cannon going off and the sounding of bugles."

Chapter 1

Farewell Batang

At Batang we were refreshed by Christian fellowship with the Edgar Nichols and Ellis Back families of the Tibetan Church of Christ Mission. However, we needed to go on as soon as possible. Batang any day might turn over to the Communists, and we still had before us two or more high mountain passes that might close with winter snows at any time. If the passes closed, we would not be able to go on for four or five months, until April or early May.

Even before we arrived in Batang, when Mr. Nichols and Mr. Back met us in the dusty trail in the canyon, we had asked them about routes and started planning our journey onward. In Batang we contacted an experienced caravan man to get us through southeast Inner Tibet. Because of the unsettled circumstances, he first asked an outlandish price for taking us and six horse loads through. However, we came to a more reasonable agreement after about five days of bargaining. Such is the custom in China.

Meanwhile, we were all making the multitudinous preparations for launching into the Salween Valley and beyond.

Discouraging Reports

We were hearing various reports that were far from encouraging. The Swiss Catholic mission property at Tsakalo on our route had been confiscated by the Tibetan lamas. When the Catholic priest tried to get through to Lhasa to appeal, he was sent for, brought back, and then shot in an ambush by the lamas. The Tibetans in the Atuntze area were reportedly preparing to go on the warpath down the Mekong and Yangtze Valleys to clean out the Communists.

The Reds from the north had come down within about eight days' journey from Batang. To the east of us, the main Communist armies had advanced within about 150 miles of Chungking. On the west, the Inner Tibetan government had driven out all non-resident Chinese from Tibet and had closed the border to anyone but citizens. Even under such circumstances, our caravan man, being himself a resident of Tsakalo in Tibet, believed he could persuade the various Tibetan officials as we went along and thereby get us through southeast Tibet into the mission area "where China, Tibet, and Burma meet."

Farewell Prayer

With clothes washed, food re-stocked, and boxes repaired, Mel and I started out from Batang on November 23, 1949. Around noon of that day, the Christians of the church of Christ at Batang, together with the Edgar Nichols and Ellis Back families, came to see us off. About a mile out of town we gathered in a circle for a farewell prayer and sang "God Be with You till We Meet Again." Then Mel and I rode off to catch up with our caravan.

Farewell, Batang

My Father's Mentor's Gravesite

As we crossed over a ridge into the main valley, far down below us was the grayish green river winding among its banks and sand bars. As we continued down-valley on the east side, we realized that just across the river was the forbidden land of Tibet. Of course, it looked the same on the west bank as on the east—steep, barren, forsaken-looking mountainsides with shriveled grass and a few scrub trees, the only vegetation to intersperse sharp, jutting rocks and cliffs. On our way we took pictures of the gravesite of Dr. Shelton, who was shot by Tibetan bandits in 1922. Then we continued rapidly, for the sun was going down and we had far to go.

Gravestones for Dr. Loftis and Dr. Albert Shelton

Chapter 2

Past Border Hurdles

On Thanksgiving Day, we crossed from collapsing Nationalist China into Inner Tibet in a large wooden barge propelled by huge four-man oars. There seemed to be only one or two Tibetan soldiers on the other side. However, the actual border military officer was in a village above the crossing. Our Tibetan caravan head went up with appropriate gifts of large bricks of coarse tea leaves and twigs to talk with him. Meanwhile, the other caravan men saddled and loaded the horses, and we continued ahead.

Wooden barge

Our caravan head caught up with us farther down the west bank of the Yangtze Valley. He said the official had put up a number of objections but was finally persuaded to let us pass. We forded a deep stream, reaching about halfway up the horses' bellies, and that night camped near some impressive, thundering rapids of the Yangtze River. The next day we turned into a branch valley of the Yangtze and headed westward away from China.

Snowy 12,000-Foot Pass

It snowed that afternoon, but we felt good because we were going onward. The third day within Inner Tibet, we proceeded through a long, cultivated valley in the jurisdiction of another Tibetan military official, the *Ja-ben*, of Pamutang. While we went ahead to a fortress-like Tibetan mud house for the night, our caravan head rode to a cluster of houses atop a hill to see the Ja-ben. The next morning, we crossed a snowy 10,000- to 12,000-foot pass into the jurisdiction of the Gonka Lama. We thought we had passed our last barrier and would have little difficulty from there on. However, we were mistaken.

Hailed to Stop

Descending through beautiful evergreen forests, that night we camped in a small ravine. About twilight, we heard the sound of horse bells coming down the road, and a military messenger passed us headed for the Gonka Lama. We had a premonition of ill tidings. About 10:00 a.m. the next morning, the fifth day of our journey, we were hailed to a stop in a Tibetan village of Dzong Tsa near the Gonka Lamasery, and a number of Tibetans gathered around us. They told us that, on orders of the Gonka Lama, we could go no farther. After we had left Pamutang, the Ja-ben had changed his mind and quickly dispatched the messenger to the Gonka Lama to stop us. At the same time, he had sent another messenger to General (*Da-ben*) Dege-Se, his superior at Gartok. We were to wait for his reply via fast military post (horseback) as to whether we could go on or not.

A Party at Our Expense

Flat-topped Tibetan mud houses, irrigated fields in the valley, and snow-topped mountains on three sides . . . Dzong Tsa was indeed picturesque. The first night, we had the experience of going to the Tibetan-style opera, unlike anything American, in our honor. We were gratified until we found that we would have to pay for it, but assented anyway.

A fiddler led. Then all the participants, singing, went whirling around in a circle with the men in one part of the circle and the women in another, by the light of piled, flaming pinewood. Occasionally they changed directions, undoubtedly to keep from getting dizzy.

"Borrow the Road"

The weather was intermittently sunshiny and cloudy, a warning that the route ahead over the mountain passes would be closed for the winter before long. At the close of the following day, the messenger from Gartok had still not arrived and we were getting impatient. The First Regent of the Gonka Lama, who had just arrived in the village, seemed friendly when we visited him. I explained our wanting to "borrow the road" through southeast Tibet to the mission area. I mentioned that my brother Robert and Betty had come from Likiang to the Mekong Valley earlier in the year with the Gonka Lama's Third Regent. That fact helped matters.

The First Regent suggested that we proceed onwards to Tsakalo and wait there for the Da-ben's reply. We thanked him for his kindness in permitting us to go to Tsakalo, which was about halfway across southeasternmost Tibet on our direct route. Seven days' journey onward was better than being compelled to retreat seven days to Batang.

Night Flight

At 2:30 a.m. we arose. The horses were saddled and loaded in the light of a flaming bundle of straw. We ate some breakfast and went stumbling through the chilly darkness, anxious lest we hear the jingling horse bells of the messenger catching up with us. Crossing an incompleted, frost-slippery bridge of three logs over a small river, we climbed up a mountain by starlight.

About dawn, one of the Tibetans found that five of the animals had strayed somewhere along the road in the darkness. After the caravan men went back and found the missing ones, we continued, climbing into a high, rocky valley of dense fir forest and surrounded by snow-capped peaks. We climbed through snow to a 12,000-foot pass over the Yangtze-Mekong Divide. Far across the huge chasm of the Mekong Valley, we could see the towering range of snowy, storm-clouded mountains forming the Mekong-Salween Divide.

That night we camped in a field several hours' journey from Tsakalo. In the morning, just as our horses were being loaded, a military horseman passed us again. As we went through a village a short distance down, he hailed us. A special military officer, sent by the General of Gartok to investigate our case, was coming. He wanted us to stop there, but we told him we could discuss everything when we arrived in Tsakalo.

Chapter 3

Halted by Tibetan Military

Shortly after we arrived at Tsakalo on December 1, we heard that the Gartok Da-ben's officer had arrived. When we went and explained that we were Americans, he was very courteous. Nevertheless, he asked us to write a letter to the Da-ben and told us that we would have to wait until a reply came. The Da-ben could read English, so I wrote explaining that we were neither bandits nor Communists, but American missionaries only wanting to cross a corner of Tibet to reach our mission area beyond the borders of Tibet. Our regular route had been cut off at Likiang by Chinese Communists, mutual enemies of Tibetans and Americans. According to Tibetan custom, I sent a gift for the general: a J. C. Penney Co. flannel shirt and a well-worn issue of the *Reader's Digest*.

108 Eggs, 72 Tangerine-Oranges, and 18 Native Pears

The next day, while waiting for the reply, we were greatly surprised to see the general's officer bringing several wooden trays piled high with 108 eggs, 72 tangerine-oranges, and 18 native pears. Figuring it would be almost impossible to carry nine dozen eggs by horseback, we fried over a dozen a day. The officer must have exhausted the community egg supply!

At noon on the eighth day of waiting, the messenger from Gartok arrived. The letter, written in Tibetan, was wrapped in the *kattah* or white ceremonial scarf used as token of high esteem and respect. He also sent us a return gift consisting of a package of canned foodstuffs—evaporated milk, condensed milk, powdered milk, California sardines, India-canned tomatoes, and Lipton's tea—and a woolen Tibetan blanket.

Da-ben Dege-Se had kindly sent a messenger to the highest officials at Chamdo to get us a pass for places outside his jurisdiction. If we should have to cross in Tibet clear to India, we should have permission. The government headquarters in Chamdo, the capital of Kam province, could give us passage from Tsakalo across the Tsawarong Valley into Brahmaputra Valley in Tibet. Thus, we could reach Sadiya in India.

Telegram

Not long after we arrived at Tsakalo, a special messenger, having come the seven days' journey from Batang, brought a telegram from my father in Kunming—the last outside news for many months. It told us all the missionaries in the Mekong and Salween Valleys of the mission area had evacuated to Burma. Thence we knew what to expect.

Detained: Guests or Prisoners?

Notwithstanding the General's friendliness, we were still stuck at Tsakalo. The best communications in Tibet were by special military messenger on horseback. The messenger should be able to make the trip faster than the 24 days it would take a caravan; however, there was no telling how long red tape in provincial headquarters might take. Officials there might not be very congenial.

We had first hoped for permission within five days; now it was almost one month. We wondered if we should have to stay the whole winter, if we would get out at all. Mel and I finally settled down to learning Tibetan, Lisu, Chinese, and Greek. We studied as much as nine hours a day. Mel also had his piano-accordion to play, and I had a chromonica, which helped our spirits considerably. Meanwhile, our every action was most suspiciously watched.

Christmas: Hanging Socks

Weeks passed; then Christmas came. To celebrate, we opened a can of sardines, some Klim [dry milk power], and Postum [coffee substitute]. I dug out one carefully saved package of chewing gum apiece and some candy, hanging them up in socks in fun. Without many-colored streetlights or Christmas music, we had a quiet Christmas Sunday. According to our custom on the Lord's Day, the two of us alone partook of the Lord's Supper, and had a bit of singing, studying, and devotions.

Chapter 4

Pseudo-Shangri-La

Tsakalo was terrifically cold and windy. At least, we were almost frozen in the one-room penthouse where we stayed. I found that long wool underwear are the scratchiest things next to "the seven-year itch." But over the flat-topped Tibetan roof we had a wonderful view of the snow mountains across the valley.

Tsakalo with mountain view

About half of the days were sunshiny. For 15 miles opposite us a range of jagged peaks rose precipitously from the valley into the deep blue sky. On full moon nights they looked impressive. With massive cliffs, jagged rocks so steep no snow could stick, but snow plentifully covering the tops, these peaks were like huge fortress walls and towers of diamond glitteringly hanging far above in the sky. Their beauty offset the dry barrenness of the rest of the valley.

One Copper Teakettle

Tsakalo itself was a slouchy village scattered over a valley shelf. Its "stores" boasted several wooden bowls, raw tobacco, and cotton yarn. One place astoundingly had a copper teakettle, but we bought that when we first arrived, and so Tsakalo lost its only major store exhibit. One can understand why most of the living had to be from sources other than store keeping. Two crops a year were produced in the fields. During December, people were planting their winter crop of barley. Because of the dryness, they had to irrigate their fields almost like the Chinese had to irrigate rice paddies.

Two Horseloads of Salt

The only item for which Tsakalo was really noted throughout this part of southeast Asia was the salt wells near the river. The people carried saltwater from the wells and poured it into mud "drying pans" on platforms overhanging the steep riverbanks. Tsakalo's notorious wind—it should be called Tibet's Windy City—helped to dry the saltwater to produce a muddy, reddish-looking salt for trade along the border areas by horse, mule, and donkey caravans. We bought two horseloads of the salt to take all the way into the Salween Valley and Burma. It turned out to be more valuable there than money.

Chapter 5

"The Gospel in Tibet?"

The lamas were the class of power in the land of Tibet. Sometimes, a large crowd of them would come to visit and hear Mel play his piano accordion. We wondered sometimes whether they were looking over our stuff and if they might ambush us as they did the Swiss Catholic priest. A number of times, various Tibetans offered to sell us clothes and other possessions of the murdered priest. We did not appreciate the irony.

"The Gospel in Tibet?"

LaVerne and lama leader

In spite of obstacles and the uncertain feeling that we might be leaving any day or not for months, after Christmas we were able to hold several preaching services in Tsakalo, Inner Tibet. Various people warned us we should not try preaching, reminding us of what happened to the Catholic priest.

It was suggested we'd better ask permission from the Gonka Lama's regent. I asked him about holding a meeting in the street. He said no, "since it would be disturbing the populace." But he grudgingly allowed us permission for several meetings in a house fronting on the street. Mel played the accordion and I spoke. We felt a good work could be done in time throughout Inner Tibet if the supreme power of the lamas were broken. Nevertheless, probably even then one would have to work many more years with fewer results than with most other peoples.

The Depths of Darkness

One cannot imagine the depths of evil and darkness in which Satan has plunged the people in this heathen stronghold. One could truly see and feel evil in their every action. They knew nothing such as love; they could not imagine such a thing as "love thy neighbor as thyself."

You who read this, tell people back in the States to be more thankful to God for the trustworthiness, peace, and love that Christ has instilled in the American life. Tell the young people of America, won't you, to cherish and strengthen the Christian principles that are the foundation of our life and hope, to do their best with all their heart and life that Christ's love might break through to these pits of darkness. America is wonderful when one realizes the comparative utter spiritual wretchedness, the shadow of death, that chokes the air of this land.

Calling All Spirits

One day we noticed a large number of lamas in the village. They had come to perform various special ceremonies, mainly the supposed driving out of evil spirits from the village for the coming year. Day after day we heard them blowing their lama horns from some house or rooftop. Sometimes there was a regular brass band. One bass horn had an unusual, odd-sounding tremble. Another horn we nicknamed the "weeping horn" because it sounded like

"The Gospel in Tibet?"

a person in anguish. A third horn was the "dying cow," a huge, low bass that would boom out over the valley. These, with occasional bursts of drumbeating and shouting and screaming, formed the preliminary rites.

One day we heard about a parade. The Lamas gathered in full dress, with tall coxcomb capes and wine-colored garments trimmed with gold. They blew the horn, clanged cymbals, and beat their drums. Other men stood on the housetops and shot off their old-fashioned muskets to scare away the devils. The lamas standing in a row starting chanting in a deep, throaty voice, then going faster and faster.

The chief lama stepped forward with pyramid-shaped effigies, each with a miniature skull on top, and one by one threw them in a flaming bundle of straw. Then all the lamas shouted, ending the ceremony, and all the devils were to be expelled from the village. One could feel the power and influence—sometime even the presence—of Satan in such an occasion. We surely thanked God that we could trust in His care.

Lama and effigy with miniature skull

Rats

Besides various other forms of rats in this area, the four-legged ones were awfully active around us during our stay there. Huge gray rats would chase all over the room at night as soon as the lantern was out. Mel complained that they were using his bed as a football field at night—with him in it.

As soon as one of us would turn on a flashlight, a bowling game began. We usually had on our table some pears and stale biscuits from Batang. Running past our heads, the rats would get onto the table and gnaw on the pears. They would have a wonderful time dragging the biscuits underneath my bed toward their rathole.

One night I got disgusted at the pestiferous persistence of the pesky things. Dragging the biscuits toward my bed, they would bang them against our kerosene tin at the head of my cot. I would awake (if I had even fallen asleep) to the hear the rats proceeding further and further with the biscuit, but whenever I turned on my flashlight, I could find no rats, only a biscuit.

Finally, I laid my Tibetan sword on a bench in easy reach from my bed. When I heard the rats towing the biscuit under my bed, I reached over quietly for the sword. All of a sudden, I thrust it under my bed and swung it back and forth with force. I was disturbed no more that night; in the morning I found the biscuit still under my bed. However, the rats continued other nights. Once, two rats got into a fight on the table. One lost his footing in the squabble, and bounced off the table unto my pillow, and made a hurried exit. Well, rats!

Chapter 6

Permission Granted!

Twenty-nine days after being stopped at Tsakalo, we heard the jingling horse bells of the official messenger from Chamdo. He had gone from the General of Gartok to provincial headquarters, a 12-day journey for caravans, in three days and nights. Thereupon, the governor at Chamdo had radioed Lhasa to ask what should be done with us. Somehow, though, the Lhasa government had taken 16 days to reply. We wondered whether it radioed our passport numbers all the way to Washington, D.C., for verification.

Finally, the reply came back that we should be given full permission to travel through Tibet to Sadiya, India. America and Tibet being allies, we should be given full travel privileges. We were to take our passports up to Gartok to get visas from the general. Then the Da-ben would assure us transportation to the borders of Tibet as guests of the Tibetan government.

On one day, we were prisoners wondering whether we'd be shot or allowed to continue; the next day, we were honored guests of the government of Tibet. We were almost shocked off our feet with the sudden good news.

Authority to Travel and Conscript Pack Animals

On January 1, 1950, Mel Byers and I left Tsakalo. We rode on horseback up the dry sandstone gorge of the Mekong, then over a ridge into a beautiful side-valley with evergreens on the mountainsides, the streams frozen solid. We traveled with the General's soldier-messenger arranging transportation. With government authority in Tibet, one travels from village to village with the public supplying the animals for transport practically free, doing this as part of their taxes or allegiance to the government.

From the Mekong Valley we crossed over a very cold pass into a branch of the Yangtze Valley. The people here were very curious to see the white strangers. Once the Tibetans asked in awe and wonder if what they had heard was actually true, that white people washed their faces regularly! On this part of our journey, we were puzzled as to why all the women had such black, dirty-looking faces in comparison with the men. We found out that they painted their faces with a mixture of soot and yak butter to protect their faces from the cold. Certainly, this was a striking type of cosmetic, but one which we thought did not improve their looks.

This part of our journey did seem colder than any place before. Even with the sun out, until about noon, we needed heavy, hooded parkas and practically everything warm we could get on underneath. The small river in the valley was also frozen. Several times the caravan of horses, yaks, cows (these are used for pack animals in Tibet), and mules crossed the river on ice.

At one place we were surprised to see the people carrying their water supply in baskets; the water was ice-chunks. Here we also saw a new invention. Above Tibetan fireplaces, there was generally a hole in the roof for the smoke to go out. At one house we saw a small windmill-type prayer wheel suspended above the fireplace so that it was turned by the smoke going up the draft.

Chapter 7

Markam Fort—Horns, Flutes, and Drums

*I*n the early afternoon of January 5, as we rode across the plain, we noticed in the distance at the foot of the surrounding mountains a fair-sized fortress with low, thick walls. A large crowd of the local populace had gathered before the entrance to witness the arrival of the first white men in 12 years. As we rode up, some Tibetan officers came out to receive us. We dismounted, turned over our horses to several soldiers, and entered the first and then the second line of fortifications. There we met the general, dressed in a wine-colored silk gown, with long, plaited hair and a long earring of turquoise set in gold. He greeted us in very good English, leading us within the third set of fortifications, his personal residence, to a room that had been prepared for us.

The luxurious surroundings in which we found ourselves so suddenly were certainly unexpected in this far-off corner of the world. One bedstead had a leopard-skin covering. Two couches in the room had beautiful, ornate wool. On the floor were Lhasa-woven rugs with richly colored lotus-flower designs.

The general's living room, where we had our three meals each day and visited with him, was likewise adorned with ornate rugs and oil-painted with various Tibetan scenes. A special servant was assigned to us and stood nearby, handing to us every few moments a fresh bowl of hot Tibetan buttered tea. The covers of the bowls were intricately wrought silver.

A Garrison Parade

Life in a Tibetan fortress at 10,000 feet altitude amidst the cold plateaus and mountains of the borderland must be like a page or a chapter out of *Beau Geste* [a 1924 adventure novel by P.C. Wren]. Early in the morning, we were awakened by the sound of lama horns, flutes, and drums. Then there was a terrific boom of a mountain cannon going off, and the sounding of bugles. We asked the general if we might take pictures of a few of the Tibetan soldiers. Thereupon, one day he gave orders for the entire garrison of Markam Fort to go on grand parade at 2:00 p.m. for our benefit.

The general dressed in full uniform and carried a long, shiny-white general's sword. Parade orders were given in English, as the soldiers had been trained in India. We were thrilled to see the rugged Tibetan soldiers dressed in their orange-wool native uniforms and fur hats. The bugle corps, the bagpipes, the large drums, and the small drums were especially colorful. For the drummers, the troops had trained the soldiers' young sons, who were tasseled with the national colors. The Tibetan national flag presented a vivid picture with its red, blue, white, yellow, and green silk. We were able to take complete Kodachrome pictures of all of this.

Markam Fort

National Geographics and Dagwood

In looking over the general's *National Geographics*, we were especially interested to read an article that mentioned the general. During the first part of World War II, two American officers, Tolatoi and Dolan, went to Lhasa as special representatives of President Roosevelt. General Dege-Se, then captain, had escorted them on the last part of their journey. Thus, he knew about Americans and highly praised Christian principles and missionaries.

All in all, we found the general astonishingly different from what one would expect at a lonely plateau outpost in a corner of Tibet. He had received his education at a school at Gyantze, Tibet, taught by an English couple. We were surprised to see in his possession Alley Oop and Dagwood comics clipped from 1947 Shanghai newspapers!

Even here in Gartok we found that the people had not forgotten the visit from my parents 25 years ago. The general had a picture of Gartok taken by my father that had been given to one of the preceding government officials.

General Dege-Se appeared sorry to see us leave. Evidently our visit had been a welcome change in the routine of a lone Tibetan fortress in southwest Tibet. Also, he had been quite ready to listen and to discuss with us the advantages of Christianity and seemed very friendly to the missionary cause. He certainly was profusely hospitable. On the day of our leaving, we found assembled outside our door a quarter of a yak, a large bag of tsamba, rice, flour, butter, cheese, biscuits, and a Lhasa-style tsamba-and-sugar cake. We had to get an extra animal to carry all the extra food. This lasted us over a month.

Chapter 8

Privileged Travelers in Tibet

On January 9, 1950, the general, with a number of his servants and soldiers, escorted us a short distance toward the pass into the Mekong Valley. After we parted and rode off westward, he continued to wave to us until he was far up the trail.

We had a cloudless day for going over the cold, grass-covered pass and descending into the dry Mekong Valley. There we saw yak herds grazing peacefully on the mountain pastures amidst tall evergreens. When we stopped for the night, we especially appreciated the privileges of traveling as guests of the Tibetan government.

One of the two soldiers sent as our escort traveled ahead into the village to prepare a room for us. As soon as we arrived, people came out to hold our horses as we dismounted; we were led upstairs in the block-styled Tibetan house, and then given as much buttered tea as we could drink. Transportation was drafted by the soldiers from one village to the next. Sometimes we had a very motley assortment of yaks, cows, horses, mules, donkeys, and people carrying our stuff.

First White Men

We were told that no white men had ever been through this particular section of the country. When we passed through villages, large crowds of men, women, and scarcely dressed children came out to stare at us fearfully from a distance. Sometimes, as we approached, some of them would run away. On a map we had of Tibet, this part of the Mekong Valley was marked with a dotted line, indicating its course was uncertain. It consisted of tremendous, almost impassable, gorges winding rockily from one sharp angle to the next.

At Sampa-dreng we saw our first Tibetan yak-skin rope bridge, a single cable of woven yak-skin strips. Here the deep turquoise Mekong River flowed placidly between 150-foot cliffs of red, yellow, black, and orange. However, since the water during this season was low, we crossed on a clumsy-looking, five-log raft. The singing of the raft men echoed between the cliffs as we crossed.

We found the people very curious, stalwart, and friendly on this part of the trip. Some of the "modesties" of civilization seemed not to have reached them, though. The children were naked. One boy of perhaps 10 years was very careful about the boots he was wearing, though he had on nothing else.

The people were very superstitious. When I wound my 35 mm film off its spool, I put my large Tibetan chupa over me in the blackness on the porch one evening, to rewind the film onto the spool. The Tibetans must have thought I was working magic. When I re-entered the house, all of them had a 15-minute chant to one of their goddesses for protection against evil.

At Tsaachorten, there was a huge Lamaist shrine, a chorten five stories high. It had 277 *mani* drums, huge skin-covered rolls of manuscripts written with the Lamaist prayer, *Om mani padme hum*. Pilgrims believed they gained merit by going through the shrine turning the 277 drums. Each time they turned a drum around, they believed they gained the equivalent merit of saying the entire number of prayers written in the scroll within.

Mani Rock Pile

From here, we looked forward to crossing the Gotreh-la Pass separating the Mekong from the Tsawarong Valley. The streams were covered with a solid sheet of ice. Here was our first casualty of the road. In crossing a patch of ice on the road, one of the lead yaks fell off the path and broke its hip. While one of the Tibetans went back to Tsaachorten for a replacement yak, we camped nearby under a cathedral of magnificent oaks and evergreens.

For the campfire, our yak drivers dragged down a huge 20-foot log. The blaze felt good in the sharp cold. The next morning after the replacement yak arrived, we came out into a huge cirque with three large frozen lakes amidst the bare rocks, huge boulder, and cliffs. At the top of this cold, 15,000-foot pass, we found the characteristic Tibetan mani rock pile. Thence we descended sharply into the Tsawarong Valley.

The following day, we saw across the valley a fair-sized town, Drayuh, with a large, white-walled lamasery and a small fort. A long wooden bridge on rock piles crossed the solidly frozen river. We had sent one of our soldiers ahead to the military commander here, with an introductory letter from General Dege-Se of Gartok. Soon after our arrival, we were visited by an elderly gentleman, representing the absent military commander, and the district civil official, bringing gifts of rice, butter, dried noodles, and brown-sugar lumps.

They tried hard to persuade us to go directly from Drayuh over two passes to the Zayul River and thence to India. They explained that the Salween River south in Yunnan was very turbulent with bandits and Communists. We finally convinced them that we had to get to the Salween Valley below, that only if it was impossible to reach there were we to continue in southeast Tibet to India.

Chapter 9

Devil Dance

The military commander's representative persuaded us to stay as special guests to attend the annual Devil Dance at the lamasery the following day. In the morning, the official led us through the large court of the lamasery, and up to the high second-story balcony overlooking the grounds. There, Mel and I were led to a high dais covered with rich Lhasa carpets. The officials, all dressed in their richest silks and fur-trimmed hats, sat on other lower seats similarly carpeted. We sat cross-legged on the dais, eating Tibetan cookies and tangerines and drinking buttered tea, while watching and taking pictures of the Devil Dance, which began below us.

This intricate ceremony was one of our strongest impressions of the actual demon worship practiced in Tibet. At one corner of the court was a silk-clad figure with a disproportionately large head who was seated on a throne with two masked dwarf attendants. Across the court from us were the lamas blowing various types of horns, beating drums, and clanging cymbals. They combined the instruments, with according high and low sounds, to accompany the scenes portrayed by the masked dancers in the court. The tempo of the horns, drums, and cymbals varied from the slow, death-like tempo of the four ghosts carrying in a bound corpse, to the frenzied tempo of the pig-headed, horned demon carving the corpse.

Devil dance performance

At first, we were quite interested in the exquisite silk costumes and the masks. We laughed at the antics of the three skull-headed clowns that played tricks on the seated audience at the edge of the court.

There were eight scenes altogether, with an intermission after the third. Each scene was heralded by a march of red-robed, tall-capped lamas with horns, a huge rod, and a sword.

The first scene was a dance by a many-weaponed king and four retainers. Then followed eight masked dancers with brightly colored silk robes. The third scene was a dance of four demon-ghosts. The skeletons and claws were grotesquely and minutely pictured on their tight garments. After the intermission, when we were given lunch, came the fourth scene of 19 demons from hell. These wore weird masks of all sorts of horrible-looking animals, their eyes staring and their horns swaying grotesquely about.

After their exit, the four demon-ghosts return for the fifth scene bearing the clay effigy of a human corpse, leaving it behind upon their departure. (In former years of lama worship, this used to be a live human sacrifice.) In the sixth scene, 13 dancers with peacock-feathered headpieces were each given cups of parched barley and buttered tea, which they poured out in sacrifice. Then one of the dancers thrust a spear into the corpse. In the seventh scene, the pig-headed, horned demon returned. Dancing to the rhythm of the drums and cymbals, this one finally kneeled before the corpse, grotesquely swaying from side to side in time with their music. The tempo grew faster and faster, and finally, the demon cut up the corpse methodically with quick strokes of a knife.

The last scene was a dance of the large-headed figure, retainers, and clowns, and their exit. By this time, we had a thorough repugnance and horror of the satanic religion of Lamaist Tibet. Surely this land is in the darkest clutches of the devil's power, within the depths of satanic fear and superstition. Oh, that the healing truth and freedom of Christ might clean out the rotten filth, superstitions, and bondage!

Rickety Wooden Cantilever Bridges

From Drayuh, we rode down the cold valley of the Tsawarong Yi-chu, a large branch of the main Salween River. The evergreens seemed to grow taller. Firs then gave way to pines. The emerald flowing river far below took the place of the ice river at Drayuh. We even saw some bamboo, alerting us to an approaching semi-tropical gorge. Rock pillars standing 2,000 feet tall formed a gateway. We had to cross and recross the river on rickety wooden cantilever bridges, then climb to the tops of 1,000-foot cliffs. Sometimes as we rode our horses, one knee might be hanging over 800 feet of almost sheer space.

We witnessed the supremacy of government in Tibet. All along this part of our trip, our two Lhasa soldiers had the job of arranging transportation from one village to the next. Each soldier had a leather-woven whip at the end of a short stick, which he used as his sign of authority. Once, one of the soldiers merely sent his whip several days' journey ahead as notice to have transport animals ready upon our arrival.

The lower Tsawarong Yi-chu River made two huge hairpin loops near its confluence with the main Salween. The valley was extremely dry. Villages seemed to consist of half a dozen or so castle-like establishments, each owned by a very rich Tibetan with all his retainers and their families living around or in the main establishment. We finally crossed the Tsawarong Yi-chu and climbed over a pass to the main valley of the Salween.

Tibet No More

You can imagine our excitement at looking down the valley and seeing, far below, the group of mountains separating us from the mission field in the Salween Valley, Yunnan Province. It seemed that we were now, at last, nearing the end of our detour from Kunming to the Lisuland field. We descended eagerly to the village of Trana, arriving there after dark by starlight. We received the impression of arriving at some medieval castle, with the flaring pine torches flickering their light against the tall stone walls of the fortress-like Tibetan house. We didn't realize it at the time, but that was to be our last regular horse or muleback ride in Inner Tibet as guests of the Tibetan government.

Looking toward the Salween Valley

Chapter 10

Bandit Territory

At Trana we talked with the first people who really seemed to know very much about a people called Lisu lower down in the Salween Valley. Apparently, the formidable series of gorges separating Tibetan country from Lisuland kept anyone except locals from having any travel interests back and forth. You can imagine how excited we were to have contact with Lisuland after so many months! The Tibetans all tried their hardest to persuade us not to go down into China, but to go over the Mekong pass to India. They said that bandits were still plundering the Salween Valley below, and that we might be killed. However, we insisted that we at least should go down to look over the situation.

Thus, we started off down the desert-like, brier-filled canyon. In several places the road was propped up on timbers around cliffs with the deep waters of the river several hundred feet below. From Songta, the last village on the Tibetan side of the border, we hired carriers to take us to Kieunatong, the northernmost village with Lisu Christians on the China side of the border.

Monkey Trail

For the first stretch through the tremendous gorges, we floated downriver in dugout canoes. Separating the Tibetan territory from Chinese territory in the Salween Valley were the terrific Marble Gorges, which take three days for carriers to go through. The cliffs sometimes went up thousands of feet from a dashing river. The trail—or rather, monkey-trail—wound around precipices on narrow ledges. At one place, it led up a cliff on about a 25-foot notched log. By this time, we were traveling altogether on foot and our equipment was being carried by porters. Here, the vegetation was dramatically changed to that of a lush tropical jungle. Elephant grass, vines hanging from leafy green trees, orchids, and ferns were a welcome change from the dry thorns and sparse grass of the lower Tsawarong.

Bandit Territory

Nung boatmen with long oars

Mel traveling through the Marble Gorges

Plunderers and Murderers Ahead

As we approached Kieunatong, we met a Tibetan trader coming north who handed us a letter addressed "To the two real or imaginary foreign travelers in Tsawarong Province." A Swiss Catholic layman, working with priests in northwest Yunnan, had heard reports of our being in Tsawarong and wanted us to send out word to Switzerland that he was safe. When we arrived at Kieunatong, we knew practically nothing of the situation in the mission area. However, when we met with the Swiss there, Mr. Chappelet, the first white man we had seen in several months besides each other, gave us a fairly complete picture.

Successive bands of Tibetan plunderers and murderers had swept through the valley. Pretending to be Nationalist soldiers fighting the Communists, they poured across the passes from the upper Mekong Valley, wantonly killing and pillaging the innocent, peace-loving Lisu tribespeople. They plundered and burned the mission house and the local church building at Pugeleh and cleaned out the belongings at the Tada station. However, about the time Mel and I arrived on the China side of the border, the final large band of robbers was reportedly preparing to leave the Salween Valley about 30 miles south of us. About eight were remaining in the valley, but Mr. Chappelet thought we could get by them all right to visit the congregations of the valley.

We headed south towards Tada, where Stephen, a Lisu preacher and an old-time special friend of mine, was reported hiding out in the mountains from the Tibetan robbers. The second day south of Kieunatong, Mel and I, together with Mr. Chappelet, met the few remaining armed bandits. We explained that we were American missionaries with special passes from the Inner Tibetan Government, with some Inner Tibetan soldiers as our escort waiting for us near the border. Sending our several loads ahead while we stayed behind and talked with the bandits, we passed without incident.

One day's journey north of Tada, we met a number of Christians of the Bipili and Sholalo congregations. Astonished, they shook hands with us heartily and wondered from where on earth we had dropped into the valley. We sent the deacon of the Bipili church to contact Stephen in the mountains above Tada. When he told Stephen and the Tada elder that Mel and I had come down from Tibetan country, they refused to believe him.

Stephen and the elder finally wrote me a letter. While they did not believe I had arrived, they asked, just in case it was true, would I please come down to Tada.

Mel and I made a fast trip down to the village of Tada. It was altogether deserted except for Stephen and some Christians who had come down to meet us; we were happy to see them. We stayed with them several days, teaching and conferring. After the strain of the past months, it was refreshing to our spirits, too, to sing Christian hymns with them in four-part harmony. We made plans for a Bible school to be held for the Salween Valley Christians if possible. Whatever the case, we should return to Trana, nine days' journey north in the Tsawarong, Tibet, to retrieve our stuff and bring it south into the care of the Lisu Christians high in the mountains, away from bandits.

Salween Valley mission area

Chapter 11

Five Stunned Brigands

We traveled in a moderately heavy snowstorm to a village a day's journey north of Tada where there was a congregation of Christians. There, hearing that the Tibetan bandits were farther north, but that they had stored plunder from the Tada mission house at a village across the river from us, I said to Mel, "Shucks, let's go get it." We recovered eight carrier loads of miscellany and had it carried to the house where we were staying.

The next day, we decided to retrieve more of our stolen stuff reported to be seen in a side valley. On our way back, we heard the bandits had returned south and were threatening to do something to us. We were really angry by this time. We had seen what the bandits had done to the valley people—burning, looting, raping, killing, as well as cleaning out the missionaries—and we had developed a thorough dislike for the brigand.

We decided to bluff the robbers. We hurried down the trail into the main Salween Valley, looking out for an ambush. Soon we met a herd of cows which the bandits had plundered and were planning to send toward the Mekong Valley. Behind them we met some of the bandits. I demanded where they thought they were going and proceeded to bawl them out (if that term is adequate) with the best words at my command in four languages, telling them they were nothing but a bunch of rotten, good-for-nothing robbers (it's always best to tell the truth) and that the time was ended for them to abuse the people.

Two Knives Versus Five Rifles: Outnumbered?

The brigands were used to having the valley people run from them in scores and seemed to be stunned. Mel and I, armed with hunting knives, had the five bandits with their five rifles outnumbered two to five. (Yes, you read that right!) Mel and I herded them into a courtyard. One bandit tried to get me to walk in front of him, but I told him to go ahead. I continued to give the bandits a verbal lashing. In the courtyard, we told the bandits they would have to stay there that night.

For a while, we stood somewhat uncertainly, still scolding them, with them and their guns "cornered," wondering what to do next. Then we told them to take the bullets out of their guns. When I started assisting them, a stunned bandit took the gun off his shoulder to accommodate me. I turned it over to a local bystander to hold. We proceeded with the rest.

Suddenly, when Mel started to take a rifle from one of the bandits, the latter backed away with his gun and Mel grappled with him. As they were tussling across the court for the gun, I grabbed a rifle and let the butt fly at the Tibetan with all my force. Finally, he let go of his gun. In short order we also stripped them of knives and bullets. Having disarmed all five bandits, we tied them with rope and copper wire, the latter which they had conveniently plundered and brought from the Tada house.

Strategizing the fate of the bandits

Ambush Set!

The chief of the bandits was still up north and was supposed to come down the next day. We set some of the local people as guards over the prisoners. To keep the chief from getting wind of developments, we set a guard on the northward roads. The following day, with about 20 local people armed with guns and crossbows, we set a beautiful ambush behind some huge boulders on the north road.

We waited for a whole day for the chief and his several companions only to capture a badly scared messenger with word for the bandits to return hurriedly north to join their chief at a Tibetan New Year's dance. When we returned to the village that evening, hundreds of Lisu, hearing of the capture of the bandits, were starting to pour in from the south with their knives and crossbows.

Chapter 12

Communist-Tibetan Football

As more Lisu kept pouring in, a few Chinese Communists with hand grenades popped into the courtyard where we were, shouting, "Don't anyone move!" They apparently thought they were putting something over on us. However, I told them it was time they were arriving; they had better take good care of the bandits we had captured.

They took the situation largely out of our hands, but because we had captured the five bandits, they appeared to be moderately civil. However, in spite of having around 1,200 "soldiers," they were reluctant to plunge northwards after the five or so remaining bandits. They forced them northward for two weeks without actively trying to capture them; the bandits then escaped into the narrow gorges between China and Tibet.

The bandits were on the west side. Our trail to Trana to get our stuff lay on the east side of the narrow gorge. We planned to avoid them by going past them by night if necessary but headed up with a number of carriers. By the time we went up, the bandits had moved almost into Tsawarong and we, crossing a high ridge instead of going along the river, avoided them. Then, just as we were leaving the border village of Songta in the Tsawarong on our way to Trana, the bandits appeared across the river. They were watching us, apparently wondering whether we were enemies or mere local people not necessarily to be shot at. We quickly warned the locals not to let the brigand pass up the river or to our side of it, and then hurried on, returning to Trana.

We now hoped to be mostly done with our troubles. However, when we arrived at Trana with our Lisu carriers, the local Tibetan official called us. Apparently one day's journey after us, 27 Communist soldiers had crossed the border into Tibet to capture the bandits. Now the Tibetan official believed positively that we had helped the Communist soldiers and were on their side. We, who had detoured about six months just to avoid the Communists from Kunming to the mission area, were not the culprits. We argued that we were good American citizens, and that we were somewhat in danger of the Communists ourselves. But the official refused to believe that we were anything but Reds and demanded that we order the soldiers back south. Otherwise, we should not be allowed to go back south, but would be taken to the border of India instead.

God Opens a Way!

Mel and I were almost willing to accept his threat of being taken to India. We were getting fed up with being a football between Communists and Tibetans. We did much praying that night. And God is always able to open a way where there seems to be an impassable wall. The next morning, the official was more reasonable. We could take our stuff part way to the border and then leave it under guard of Tibetan soldiers while we went to the border village of Songta to try to persuade the Communists to return south.

We hiked there in double-quick time. Mel developed blood poisoning in his leg and became rather weak, but he stopped that with sulfanilamide. Reaching Songta, we told the Communists that 500 Tibetan soldiers, all armed with guns (not crossbows and knives), were forming to come south. This was reportedly true, too. The bandits, meanwhile, had escaped. Anyhow, the Communists, half of whom were merely Lisu going after the bandits, beat a fast retreat.

Mel and I, as we returned north, were still doubting that we'd get out alive. However, as soon as the Tibetan official was convinced that we were telling the truth and were on a legitimate journey, we were extended the same courtesies we had received in other places. We then wasted little time getting into the Salween Valley south of the border with the rest of our equipment.

End Detour

The day we finally reached Tada, the Communists finished executing a number of bandits and accomplices at nearby Sukin village. It was not exactly a savory atmosphere. However, we hoped to be able to work among the churches for several months at least. The Tada house was piled inside four feet deep with the rubble left by the plundering. With the help of Stephen and other faithful Lisu Christians, we cleaned out enough of the house to make room for ourselves.

It was just about six months since we had left Kunming on September 15, 1949, on the detour through Szechwan Province, Sikang Province, Batang, and through southeast Inner Tibet to Lisuland churches in the Salween Valley. Our clothes had patches, our travel bags had large holes in them, and even the yak-skin coverings over our boxes had been worn off at the corners.

Coming across the border the last time, our diet had degraded from tsamba and buttered tea to half-rotten pork and boiled cornbread dough, so we were ready for Stephen's more civilized cooking. And we were certainly ready for a little rest—and time for a bit of diversion such as picking gray hairs out of our heads.

We heard that the several bandits who had escaped, upon getting back to the Mekong, had the most fantastic stories of how we defeated them. Up and down the Salween, too, rumors traveled that when we pointed our hunting knives at anyone, he was powerless to move hands or feet. Also, we were supposedly bullet-proof. For a while we were glad to let our reputed magic lie unexhibited.

Mainly, we were glad to arrive where we were most needed. With Communists threats and plundering bandits, the Christians needed all the encouragement possible. Many of those in the Salween had stood admirably faithful despite all trials. Some were brokenhearted and bewildered at their own failings and the confusion around them and before them. They needed a lot of teaching, love, and exhortation to be set back on their feet.

The Christians needed encouragement to stand faithful in impending difficulties. The churches needed to be set again in order, and to be started on a working plan under the new and more difficult situations they would likely face. Once started, they could probably keep on quite well in spite of persecutions.

We certainly seemed to have reached the place where we were needed most at the right time. We thanked God for a safe ending of our detour through Tibet. Pray for us that we may ever trust Him! May we always be instruments held in His hands for His use.

PART VI
The Salween Valley

"Mel and I had a good opportunity for boosting morale, teaching, and making plans for the Christians here...."

"The Communists are going strong on teaching their doctrine up and down the Salween Valley. They are regularly using the chapel building at our former station to teach Communist doctrines on Sundays. They put up pictures of Stalin and Mao Zadong and demand that everyone bow his head before the pictures..."

Chapter 1

The Salween Situation

Right now, the fate of 2,000–4,000 Christians in the Salween Valley is at stake, and the time limit for action seems short. During the past several months following our capture of the five Tibetan bandits in the upper Salween Valley on February 10, Mel and I had a good opportunity for boosting morale, teaching, and making plans for the Christians here. However, with the recent opening of the passes and the resumption of traffic in and out of the valley, outside Communists have been coming in and pressure on Christians is increasing.

Valley Tours

Mel and I have been in the Salween for two and one-half months. We have had a busy and, I believe, fruitful time. We started a tour of all the congregations clear to the extreme southern end of the valley. Going from congregation to congregation, we found the Christians at first needing all the encouragement we could give them. They were terribly discouraged in not being able to continue work with the same conditions as in previous years.

Traveler on a bamboo raft

We attended the Southern Salween Easter Convention. In former years the attendance would be as high as 600–800. This time it was about 120. The drop was due to the spring epidemic of measles and pneumonia going around as well as the unsettled damage caused by the Tibetan bandits and the entrance of the Communist troops. However, after our encouragement, there seems to be a new hope, and a new spirit to grow and work in all the churches.

At another convention, this new spirit of hope and energy was manifested in the attendance of about 350. Of course, this is only about one third of the attendance of former years. However, from all directions were reports of new people turning to Christ. On Saturday afternoon during the convention, 64 people were baptized in the olive-green waters of the Salween River at the sandy beach. Thirty or more people in one area and practically an entire village in another location wanted someone to come teach them. Thus, it seems there was the beginning of a full-scale revival of the Christians, and, a turning of non-Christians all up and down the Salween Valley.

Baptisms in the Salween River

Chapter 2

Adverse Ideas

I have learned that these new ideas are being taught by the new Communist Chinese regime.

1. *Christians, being the only ones who can read and write, will be compelled to translate and teach Communist doctrine, which includes the belief that there is no God.* This would be to work against God and the gospel, wouldn't it?

2. *Compulsory public meetings will be held on Sundays.* This is a nuisance persecution against the Christian as they want to be listening to the Word of God instead. Will future Christian meetings have to be held in secret?

3. *Training of all children according to Communist doctrine.* At first, this is supposed to take the

form of compulsory education of children in Communist-approved and operated day schools. Eventually, all children six months after birth are to be given over to the state to train away from and without the consent of parents.

4. *Communal ownership of everything.* Food is to be dispersed daily from common food warehouses by officials appointed by the higher Communist officials. Thus, it would seem that the public would get only what the state deemed necessary for existence after it had put aside first whatever necessary to carry on its government and military plan.

The present statements are that for the next five years, what normal people ate in three days should be stretched to five days. To people having near starvation each spring anyway, this program sounds like more skinny bones.

Furthermore, communal ownership is meant to mean also, in the future, "communal ownership" of family relationships. Stated, "not my family, not your family, everybody's family."

All this seems to mean a breakdown of everything that Christianity and democracy uphold, a destruction of the noble, old-time ideals of respectability and decency generally to be one's goals, hopes, and/or the heart of one's honor!

5. *The requirement of a pass for travel between all areas, even local.* Thus, eventually even travel from one village to the next would require a pass from Communist officials. Wouldn't this be a very definite check on the carrying on of Christian work?

I have been trying to get a reliable picture of possible Communist activities to know what to be prepared for, and what the Christians should be ready and prepared to meet. The Communists don't need to be the only ones to make plans.

Grain Taxation

The local people aren't very happy about their liberation government. The tax assignment is 70 percent of all grain to the government granary. In a year, all fields are supposed to be divided equally. All the people are supposed to be arranged in work gangs with overseers to make sure they work hard. Eventually, it seems the Communists want to arrange it so that all food will be dispersed from the granary as the officials think necessary.

There is to be a group called the "local protection" troops. The people are to maintain a permanent garrison of soldiers from outside. In addition, the Sukin Council stated that "liberation troops to free new areas" are also to be maintained. In Yunnan (9,000,000 population), this would amount to 400,000 troops.

Pseudo Freedom

There is a lot of baloney about the oppression of the nationalists from which the Communists have come to liberate the people. Under the nationalists, it was said, there was no freedom of speech. But under the new regime, full freedom of speech was granted, and anyone could do what he wanted. However, it was warned in another part of the program that the people should watch they said about the Communist government, lest they bring trouble upon themselves. It was also said that people were to have freedom of religion. But, in other parts of the program, it was stated that everyone had to follow the Communist policy fully. With the anti-theistic declaration previously mentioned, the statement of religious freedom seems more eyewash than truth.

The Communists are going strong on teaching their doctrine up and down the Salween Valley. They are regularly using the chapel building at our former station to teach Communist doctrines on Sundays. They put up pictures of Stalin and Mao Zadong and demand that everyone bow his head before the pictures, but so far, the elders have said that they cannot bow to a picture of a person.

I have instructed the churches to not have persons officially and publicly called preachers and elders. Also, when someone must leave, someone to take his place should be appointed, but without the knowledge of the Communists. In such a way, I think that the churches can carry on their work in spite of the persecution. Our job is to help them as much possible to weather the storm.

Protecting the People

Before this Sukin Council, we had discussed that it is not right for Christians to help in any way to further the Communist doctrines, especially since they embody atheism in their present form. We have heard that two preachers we value were on the list to be compelled to teach Communism and to prepare Communist books in their language. Hence, we have arranged for their disappearance. We have heard since that the Communists, finding out that the two were gone, said they will send soldiers to force the church to work for the new government. This seems to mean that all Christian leaders will either have to work underground or will have to slip out to more convenient regions.

Chapter 3

Final Detour Through Danger

One day as Mel and I were attending the mandatory indoctrination meetings, native friends informed me that one of them had overheard plans by the Communists to capture Mel and me. Immediately we said our good-byes and headed toward Burma to meet the rest of the family.

Communist indoctrination meeting

[Editorial note: Years later LaVerne learned that this man who warned him was arrested by the Communists and put in prison for 10 years for warning him and was given an additional 10 years for another made-up charge. After 20 years, he was released. LaVerne had the chance to meet him again in the year 2000 in China and experience a heartfelt reunion.]

Crossing the Burma Border and Reunion

After crossing the river we arrived at Nyitadi, Burma. There we met my brother Robert and David Rees who had been traveling and encouraging the churches on the Burma side and doing language study and translation work in Rawang. How good it was to see their faces again! I hadn't seen Robert since I was best man in his wedding back in the U.S. several years ago.

We have enjoyed good Christian fellowship during the past several months. Faithful friends, please pray that God might lead each step of the way and that we will have the courage and ability to follow. I hope that there will be at least one more year in which we can work unhampered here in Burma.

The path ahead through governmental barriers, international dangers, and uncertainty has many times seemed blocked, with no way of going forward. Yet, as ambassadors for Christ, we have had His promise, "Lo, I am with you always, even unto the end of the world" [Matthew

28:20, KJV]. The exhortation for Joshua has been a source of assurance to us: "Be strong and of a good courage; be not afraid, neither be thou dismayed: for the Lord thy God is with thee whithersoever thou goest" [Joshua 1:9, KJV].

Epilogue

By early May 1950 all the Morse family and co-workers were relocated to Northern Burma except Ruth Margaret, who was in the U.S.; Anzie, who died from typhus on the journey; and J. Russell, who was still in China.

The mission team thus consisted of Gertrude Morse and Drema Esther; Eugene, Helen and David; Robert, Betty, and Jonathan; Isabel Dittemore and Janet; David, Lois, Warren, and Emeris Rees; Jane Kinnett; Dorothy Sterling; and LaVerne Morse and Mel Beyers.

Muladi-Putao area of Northern Burma

Tiliwago in Northern Burma

Meanwhile, J. Russell Morse was still in Kunming, China. When the last of the family left on December 7, 1949, he had planned to follow the on the next day's charter flight, but that flight didn't happen. J. Russell thus had to continue his mission work alone. When the Communists bombed near the area he lived, he provided refuge to the victims of the warfare and supplied medical needs to many who were hurt in the fighting. He helped start a school for orphans since hundreds of parents were committing suicide, leaving their children helpless. After more than a year of ministry that saw more than 250 baptisms, he was arrested by the Communist army on March 22, 1951, and placed in a Communist prison in solitary confinement where he was tortured for the next 15 months.

Without explanation, J. Russell was released from prison on June 20, 1952, and was escorted to China's

Epilogue

Bamboo Curtain border to cross the 150-yard "no man's land" separating China and the free world. He passed over to Hong Kong on his own. In Hong Kong he telephoned a missionary friend for help and received this good news: his wife Gertrude and son LaVerne were in the city at that moment! They had come from Burma to Hong Kong to see if there was any news of him before they continued to the U.S. It was a joyful reunion. After a time of rest in the U.S., they returned to Burma.

J. Russell reuniting with Gertrude and LaVerne

The Morse family, along with native Christians, continued their work of evangelism up and down the mountains of Northern Burma for many years unhindered. They shared the love of God through the development of schools and Bible training centers, language and literature production, training in music and agriculture, and providing medical services. They continued their ministry in Northern Burma until the country began closing its doors to westerners in the mid-1960s. LaVerne, with his wife Lois and their children, returned to the U.S. in 1964. He served 22 years as a missions professor at the Cincinnati Bible Seminary. He established a new mission that is now called Asia Christian Services. He wanted to encourage the key leaders that were left behind in Burma, and urge them to go south in Burma to still-unreached tribes. Almost every year he would return to Asia for six weeks to two months to encourage them and strategize with them to further expand the work. The rest of the Morse family, after going through the "Hidden Valley" years, relocated to Thailand, and have continued an extensive, expanding, and fruitful work to this day.

2021 celebrated 100 years since LaVerne's father and mother went to Asia in 1921. What started as a small "seed of faith" on the part of J. Russell and Gertrude grew and flourished. Over the years local evangelists from many tribes took the gospel into many dangerous areas in China, Burma, India, and Thailand. These evangelists went over and through mountains, valleys, plains, jungles, and rivers to find listening ears just waiting for the message.

Epilogue

Today, there is a vast number of believers—hundreds of thousands—and scores of well-trained church leaders. The work has become a movement because the love of God compels!

> *May our Lord Jesus Christ himself and God our Father, who loved us and by his grace gave us eternal encouragement and good hope, encourage your hearts and strengthen you in every good deed and word. (2 Thessalonians 2:16–17, NIV)*

> *Now to him who is able to do immeasurably more than all we ask or imagine, according to his power that is at work within us, to him be glory in the church and in Christ Jesus throughout all generations, for ever and ever! Amen. (Ephesians 3:20–21, NIV)*

About R. LaVerne Morse

Russell LaVerne Morse born in 1929 to missionaries and grew up in China. He became separated from his parents during WWII and ended up in the United States. While he was at college in the U.S. in 1949, Communism was on the doorstep of completely taking over China. His father wrote asking that he join them as they made exit plans to venture west out of danger.

After the incidents in this journal, LaVerne would return to Burma with his bride, Lois, and serve for 10 years. He then became a missions professor and pursued a new mission focusing on Burma, Thailand, and surrounding areas. He and Lois had five children and many grandchildren. He spiritually mentored and guided Christian leaders around the world. LaVerne was greatly loved and was known in Asia as *M. Pha Joseph*, or "Teacher Joseph."

LaVerne always traveled with a camera on his shoulder. He hoped that one day his six-month adventure in China would be put into print. Now, 70 years later, it has become a reality.

Marcia Morse Odor, LaVerne's firstborn, grew up with her siblings in the Muladi Village near Putao in Northern Burma. Archiving her father's writings and photos, she compiled this book as a work of love to honor her father's legacy.

More About the Morse Family

A comprehensive and compelling story of the Morse family mission from 1921–1965 is presented in the book *The Dogs May Bark: But the Caravan Moves On* by Gertrude Morse (edited by Helen Morse). *Exodus to a Hidden Valley* by Eugene R. Morse details the family's experience from 1965–1972.

Visit asiachristianservices.com to learn about the work of LaVerne and Lois Morse that continues in Southeast Asia.

CPSIA information can be obtained
at www.ICGtesting.com
Printed in the USA
LVHW100839020123
736251LV00028B/829